LCA 1375

GREAT BATTLES

GREAT BATTLES

General Editor: Christer Jorgensen

Bath • New York • Singapore • Hong Kong • Cologne • Delhi
Melbourne • Amsterdam • Johannesburg • Auckland • Shenzhen

First published by Parragon in 2011

Parragon
Queen Street House
4 Queen Street
Bath BA1 1HE, UK

Editorial and design by
Amber Books Ltd
Bradley's Close
74–77 White Lion Street
London N1 9PF
United Kingdom
www.amberbooks.co.uk

Project Editor: Michael Spilling
Design: Hawes Design
Picture Research: Terry Forshaw
Text: Martin J. Dougherty, Michael E. Haskew,
Christer Jorgensen, Chris Mann, Chris McNab,
Michael Neiberg, and Michael Pavkovic

ISBN: 978-1-4454-2474-3

Printed in China

Picture Credits

All illustrations & maps © Amber Books Ltd.

AKG Images: 16/17 (Peter Connolly), 32/33 (Muzeum Warmii Mazur)
Art-Tech/Aerospace: 43, 45, 52b, 58, 60b, 67b, 74t, 76t, 85t, 85b, 91t, 93b
Art-Tech/MARS: 28t, 51b, 56/57, 83b
Bridgeman Art Library: 35b, 37 (Agra Art, Warsaw)
Cody Images: 84
Corbis: 6 & 7 (Bettman), 13b & 34t (Bettmann), 40/41 (Bettmann), 48/49 (Fine Art Photographic Library), 52t (Adam Woolfitt), 75b
Nik Cornish: 80/81
Mary Evans Picture Library: 8/9, 10, 26
Getty Images: 24/25 & 42b (Hulton Archive), 44t (Stock Montage), 59tr (Imagno), 64/65 & 66b (MPI)
Heritage Image Partnership: 12t (Spectrum Colour Library), 50t (City of London Libraries & Guildhall Art Gallery), 53 & 59tl (Ann Ronan Picture Library), 75t (Ann Ronan Picture Library)
Library of Congress: 3, 68b, 69, 88/89, 90t
Photos 12: 18 & 20b (ARJ), 72/73 & 76b (ARJ), 77 (Oasis)
TopFoto: 90b (Topham Picturepoint)
Ukrainian State Archive: 5, 82

CONTENTS

INTRODUCTION

Warfare is all about striking a decisive blow to defeat your enemy for political or strategic reasons. At some point in a conflict, a war is decided by the outcome of a single, or series of, battles with the foe.

However, even a series of crippling blows such as those that Napoleon and Hitler inflicted upon Russia never proved decisive, since they failed to secure ultimate victory against a determined foe. For a battle to be decisive, it must lead to ultimate victory in the political or strategic sense. A great victory, however emphatic, over an undefeated enemy is never decisive if it fails to secure that ultimate victory. Some of the battles included in this volume were decisive, such as Marathon and Hastings, while others are great battles because they contributed in some way toward an ultimate victory—Trafalgar, Gettysburg, and Stalingrad were of this type. All of the battles in this volume are great clashes of arms that altered the course of history in some way.

BATTLES THAT CHANGED HISTORY

Any such list of battles will be highly selective and perhaps haphazard. The battle of Marathon is a classic great battle since it pitted democratic, western or European Greece represented by Athens against the autocratic, Asiatic empire of Persia. Yet Athens built an empire around the Delian alliance with ruthless and oppressive methods quite alien to the sophisticated and often tolerant Persians. Had the Persians won, Greece would have become more closely tied to the Middle East and not the easternmost outpost of European civilization.

This book also includes two classic Medieval encounters, from western and eastern Europe: Hastings and Tannenberg. While Hastings is one of the best known battles of all time, Tannenberg lingers in undeserved and relative obscurity outside the historical consciences of present-day Poland and Lithuania. By defeating Harold Godwinson and his insular Saxons at Hastings, Norman duke William the Conqueror tied England more closely to the European mainland, arguably helping the British Isles to become a more outward-looking country with the rich language, culture, and history that spans the globe today. Tannenberg was just as decisive a battle. Had the Polish-Lithuanian army been defeated it would have spelled the end for their Commonwealth state and meant their reduction as

BELOW: THE SCOTS GREYS' CHARGE into the center of the French line at Waterloo has gone down in the annals of great cavalry encounters. Waterloo ended Napoleon's chances of reestablishing himself as emperor of France.

vassals of the Germanic Teutonic Order. This would have altered the balance of power in Eastern-Central Europe and brought about a confrontation between Germany and Russia well before the great clash of arms in 1914.

The same holds true of the Armada expedition of 1588. Philip II of Spain was quite right to concentrate upon England and its invasion as the solution to his strategic problems. Had his ships prevailed and been able to escort the Duke of Parma's army to the southern coast of England, then truly the course of European and world history would have changed. Spain would have been able to maintain her imperial supremacy far longer than 1650 with a possibly Catholic England at her side against the other great powers in Europe, France and the Ottoman Turks.

Trafalgar was just as great a battle. The French and Spanish navies suffered a massive, crippling blow from which they were unable to recover even a century later. Nelson's victory had permanently removed the threat of a Napoleonic invasion of England while establishing British naval preponderance until the rise of the Imperial German navy 90 years later.

DECISIVE BATTLES, DECISIVE CONSEQUENCES

The battle of Waterloo is only great because it marked the final, decisive defeat of Napoleon and the end of almost an entire century of war between Britain and France for the supremacy of the world. Coupled with Trafalgar, Waterloo made the final British victory over her historical foe so much the greater. The outcome of the war against France in 1815, if not the battle itself, was never in doubt given the Allies' superior numbers and the war weariness of the French army.

The same holds true of Gettysburg. The Confederacy was far inferior in terms of manpower, industrial muscle, and resources compared to the Union side. Gettysburg was the great turning point in the Civil War, since the hitherto victorious Confederate General Lee was decisively halted in an attempt to invade Pennsylvania and split the Union in two. The Confederates were hoping that the disunited North would split and Lincoln would be forced by the appeasers to sue for a compromise peace. Truly the development of democracy, abolition, and modern America was saved on the battlefield of Gettysburg.

Much the same applies to the two twentieth century battles in our selection. The previously all-conquering Germans became bogged down and outsmarted at Stalingrad by a determined foe and by Hitler's narrow-minded obsession with capturing the city and cutting the Soviet Union's River Volga lifeline. The Soviets had by now weakened the invaders sufficiently and held the initiative from late December 1942. The Soviet pincer offensive, trapping the German Sixth Army, was a brilliant and classical military maneuver that marked the beginning of a relentless Red Army offensive westward that would culminate in the capture of Berlin in April 1945. However, as long as the Germans were holding Western Europe in their iron grip there could be no final victory against the Nazi regime. The D-Day landings in June 1944 were a huge gamble that paid off thanks to bad weather, good planning, huge resources, bold action, and German mistakes. Had German intelligence been able to discover where and when the Allies would land they could have moved troops from Pas de Calais to Normandy. This may not have been enough to change the course of the battle but if the landings had failed it would have altered the course of the war and the eventual size of the Allied and Soviet occupation zones in Europe, having massive ramifications for the post-war European political landscape.

ABOVE: ALTHOUGH ULTIMATELY achieving very little, the forceful charge of Pickett's Confederate infantry against the Union center at the battle of Gettysburg in 1863 has gone down in military folklore for its dash and bravery.

Decisive or not, the conflicts included in ***Great Battles*** have been selected because they were the great battles of their age. In some way, the outcome of each impacted on the course of world history.

Christer Jörgensen, General Editor

MARATHON 490 B.C.E.

At Marathon, an outnumbered force of Greek hoplites seized a chance to defeat their Persian foes, exploiting their superior armor and discipline to win one of the most famous tactical victories of the Ancient World. It was, however, not the end of the Persian threat to the independent Greek city-states.

By 539 B.C.E. the Persians under Cyrus the Great had conquered much of Anatolia, including those Greeks living in Ionia on the coast. Initially, relations between the Persians and their Greek subjects were relatively cordial. Over the course of the next several decades a number of tensions emerged, which soured that relationship. The Persians impeded the Greeks' economic development with trade restrictions. Moreover, the autocratic Persians imposed puppet tyrants on the Ionian city-states—something antithetical to the independent-minded Greeks. In 499 B.C.E. the Ionians finally broke into open revolt against the Persians. Their leader, Aristagoras of Miletus sought aid from the states on the Greek mainland. His first

MARATHON FACTS

Who: Nearly 11,000 Athenians and Plataean hoplites, led on the day of the battle by the Athenian general Militiades, were opposed by a multi-ethnic Persian army numbering perhaps 25,000, under the command of the Persian Artaphernes and the Median noble Datis.

What: The Athenians weakened the center of their line and strengthened their wings, allowing the Persians to push through the center, only to be defeated on the flanks and have their center enveloped by the victorious wings of the Greek army.

Where: The Plain of Marathon, about 26 miles (41.8km) from Athens.

When: August 12, 490 B.C.E.

Why: The Persians wanted to attack Athens to punish the city for its support for the rebellion of the Ionian Greek cities.

Outcome: The Persians were driven from Greece for 10 years.

LEFT: AT THE BATTLE OF MARATHON MILITIADES, with 10,000 Athenian and 400 Plataean hoplites, defeated a Persian force nearly double their size, including 10,000 Immortals, proving the value of the phalanx infantry formation.

attempt to secure allies was with Sparta. The Spartans had the best army in Greece and so were a good choice. Unfortunately, King Cleomenes did not see how sending forces to fight for the far-off Ionian Greeks was in the Spartans' interest and so declined to support the revolt. Aristagoras received a better reception at Athens. He made a speech to the Athenian assembly where he argued that the Persians were inferior to the Greeks in battle and that the wealth of the great empire would provide much loot for the victors. The assembly debated the issue and decided to send aid to their Ionian cousins—a squadron of 20 warships. The Greek armada put in at Ephesus where its troops were landed. The army proceeded to the Persian capital, Sardis, and the city was quickly taken and, with a Persian army approaching, burned to the ground. In a subsequent battle, the Greeks were defeated and the Athenians decided to return home. The revolt continued until 493 B.C.E. but the result was a foregone conclusion—the powerful and centralized Persian armed forces outclassed the individualistic Greek states in fighting a protracted war.

BELOW: THE BATTLE OF MARATHON ended dramatically with the collapse of the Persian line and a flight to the beached Persian ships. Only seven of the Persian ships escaped capture. Herodotus numbered the Persian dead at 6,400.

Although the revolt had been successfully suppressed, the great Persian king, Darius I, had learned about the participation of the Athenians and was livid. A story by Herodotus recounts how Darius had a slave tell him "Master, remember the Athenians" three times before dinner lest he forget to punish them for their interference. And so, in 492 B.C.E. Darius sent an expedition under his son-in-law Mardonius to do just that but hostile tribesmen in Thrace and bad weather off Mount Athos, necessitated the forces' return home.

THE CAMPAIGN

But Darius was not going to give up on his plans for punishing the Athenians. Thus in the following year another expedition was being prepared. This would move across the Aegean to punish the Athenians and Eretrians, who had also supported the revolt, by burning their cities and enslaving the populations. This force would be totally transported by sea, thereby avoiding the problems that had beset Mardonius' expedition. The naval component of the expedition was composed of nearly 600 ships. Perhaps 200 of these were warships serving as the fleet's escort while the remaining 400 were transports that would carry the troops and their supplies. The transports included a number of specially designed horse transportations to carry the mounts for the Persian cavalry. The landing force numbered perhaps 25,000 fighting men including a small cavalry contingent, probably about 1,000 strong. This force was commanded by Darius' nephew Artaphernes and Datis, a nobleman of Median descent. Also present was Hippias, who had ruled Athens as a tyrant until he was expelled in 510 B.C.E. The Persians understood the fractious nature of politics in a Greek city-state and no doubt saw the potential of using Hippias to raise a fifth column within Athens itself.

The Persian fleet set sail from Tarsus and sailed westward. The armada put ashore at a number of islands along the way and reduced them either through the threat or the use of force. A major landing was made on the island of Euboea in order to attack the city of Eretria, singled out, along with Athens, by Darius for punishment on account of their role in supporting the Ionian revolt. The people of Eretria were in a quandary as to what to do in the face of such a powerful force.

Some were in favor of trying to hold the town while others argued for abandoning the city and continuing to fight from nearby hills. But before a decision could be made the town was handed over by a faction who had been bribed with Persian gold in exchange for opening the gates of the town to the enemy. The temples of the city were burned in retribution for the destruction at Sardis. From Euboea the Persians headed to Attica, landing at the plain of Marathon on August 5, nearly 26 miles (41.8km) from Athens. The landing spot was undoubtedly chosen in consultation with Hippias since it provided everything the Persians required, including a long beach where their ships could be brought ashore, an ample water supply, access to Athens, and room to maneuver, especially for their cavalry, should the Athenians choose to give battle there.

When the Athenians learned of the Persians' landing, they immediately sent for aid—the herald Philippides' most famously ran 140 miles (225.3km) to Sparta. Unfortunately, the Spartans were not able to send help on account of a religious festival, the Carneia, which would not allow them to march until August 12. With this news, the Athenians debated their course of action. Some were in favor of preparing for a siege—although given Hippias' presence and the treachery at Eretria, this seemed rather risky. Others argued that it was imperative to keep the Persians penned in at Marathon and not allow them to reach the city. Included in this group was the general Militiades. His opinion carried some weight since he had previous dealings with the Persians and had fought in the Ionian revolt. As a result, the Athenian army of nearly 10,000 hoplites, heavily armed infantry, marched out to Marathon. They were joined by a force of between 600 and 1,000 hoplites from the city of Plataea, a longtime ally of Athens.

DISPOSITIONS

The Persians hauled their ships ashore along a narrow strip of beach known as the Schoinia, beyond which lay an expanse of marsh. Beyond the marsh was a village with a large area of open ground that was near a spring and it is here the Persians seem to have made their main encampment because it would have provided them with water and fodder. The Athenians and their Plataean allies encamped at the southern edge of the Plain of Marathon north of a small marsh, the Brexisa, between some high ground and the sea. The Greeks protected their camp using fallen trees with specially sharpened branches.

THE BATTLE

The two armies faced each other for perhaps four days. Each side had good reason to wait. For the Athenians, each day that passed brought Spartan aid closer—with the end of the Carneia on August 12, the Spartans would be able to march to their aid arriving perhaps by the 15th. Moreover, given the large expanse of the Plain of Marathon, and the ability of the Persians to deploy and maneuver their cavalry there, it did not make tactical sense for the Greeks to march out of the favorable terrain near their fortified camp, which was situated between the sea and the hills. This would make the heavily armed hoplites, in their phalanx formation, a formidable force against the more lightly equipped Persians. For their part, the Persians also had reason to believe that

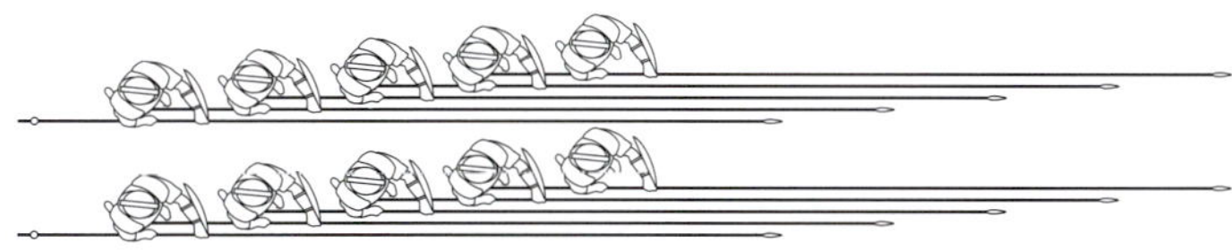

ABOVE: AN ACCURATE GREEK phalanx formation cannot be determined from ancient sources. This drawing shows one possibility, with the hoplon attached to the soldier's left arm and the spear held in both hands.

time was on their side, at least initially. As had occurred at Eretria, they hoped for help from within the city itself. In this case, they expected the supporters of Hippias to betray the city to them, no doubt with the encouragement of Persian gold. The Persians were waiting for the signal, a highly polished bronze shield would be flashed from Mount Pentele, which would indicate that all was ready.

While the details of the plan are not known, it seems clear that the Persians would embark the bulk of their troops on ships and sail to Athens while the Athenian forces were still at Marathon. Moreover, the Persians did not wish to assault the Athenians and Plataeans while in their strong position at the southern end of the plain since the terrain would nullify both their numerical advantage and the mobility of their cavalry.

By the evening of August 11, however, time was running out for the Persians. There had been no shield signal from the fifth column in Athens and the Spartan festival would be coming to an end shortly. That meant that the Athenians

GREEK HOPLITE

A typical hoplite of the Persian War era. His primary weapon was a long iron-headed spear, which could be between 6–10ft (2–3m) in length. It was usually held overarm in combat, and underarm when maneuvering. He also carried a short sword about 2ft (60cm) in length, made of iron with bronze fittings. The sword was used in both a cutting and thrusting motion. For protection he carries a hoplon (shield) made of wood with a bronze face and leather inner lining. The hoplon was secured to the hoplite's forearm by a band, and he held a grip in his left fist. His Corinthian helmet is topped with a plume of horsehair, which could be dyed for effect. His torso is protected by a cuirass of stiffened linen with metal scales added for greater protection. On his shins are molded bronze greaves, while simple leather sandals are worn on his feet.

ABOVE: RELIEF OF IMMORTALS at the Apadana, Persepolis, Iran. The Immortals were an elite royal guard within the Achaemenid Persian army. Only ethnic Persians or Medeans could be members of the unit which, according to the Greek historian Herodotus, always numbered precisely 10,000 men.

could expect Spartan reinforcements and the presence of such tough, well disciplined hoplites would dramatically transform the military balance on the Plain of Marathon. As a result, the Persians began to embark a part of their forces on the transports so they could sail for Athens the next morning while the remainder of their forces kept a watch on the Athenian and Plataean hoplites at Marathon. Even without the shield signal, the Persians could hope for help from within the city if the army were away.

This force was to be under the command of Datis and seems to have included the majority of the cavalry who would be very useful in making a dash for Athens once the task force made landfall at Phaleron Bay. Artaphernes would stay at Marathon and maintain a close blockade of the Athenian camp. He probably had about 15,000 men with him, almost exclusively infantry. Fortunately for the Athenians, they were alerted to the Persian plan by some sympathetic Ionians who were serving with the Persians. They sent the famous message "the cavalry are away," which galvanized the resolve of the Athenian commanders to offer battle. Indeed, the 10 Athenian strategoi, generals elected from each of Athens' 10 tribal divisions, were deadlocked as to whether or not to stay put and fight, return to Athens (they, too, were mindful of treachery from within the city), or to offer battle, a course of action favored by Militiades.

Fortunately, the War Archon (a ceremonial position in which the holder can cast the deciding vote in the case of such a deadlock) supported staying at Marathon and advancing against the Persians. The decision was made to launch an attack at dawn. If they could quickly and decisively defeat Artaphernes' troops it would be possible to make a forced march along the coastal road to Athens and arrive before the Persian assault force.

The next morning saw the opposing forces arrayed for battle. Militiades, who understood Persian tactics, was in command that day, and deployed the Greek forces. He knew the Persians were likely to put their best troops in the center of their battle line and that the Persian numbers would make it likely that if he arrayed his phalanx eight-deep along the entire front, they would be outflanked. In order to prevent this he made the center of his line thinner, knowing that the Persians would initially have success there.

However, Militiades also knew that the wings of the Persian formation would be formed from lighter-armed and less enthusiastic levies and that the heavily armed wings of the Greek army would be victorious. He therefore ordered that the wings not pursue the defeated levies but once they had been driven off, to wheel inward on the Persian center. The right wing was under the command of the War Archon Callimachus and the left was formed by the Plataeans.

Artaphernes deployed his troops as Militiades had expected. His best troops, Iranian soldiers from the standing army and tough Saka mercenaries, formed the center of his formation with various levies, including unenthusiastic Ionian Greeks, on the flanks. In order to maintain his close

BELOW: CLASSIC HOPLITE HELMETS, from left to right: a simple Corinthian helmet; the classic Corinthian design with long cheek pieces; a later Illyrian helmet; and a late Corinthian design with a space cut out for the wearer's ears to improve their hearing.

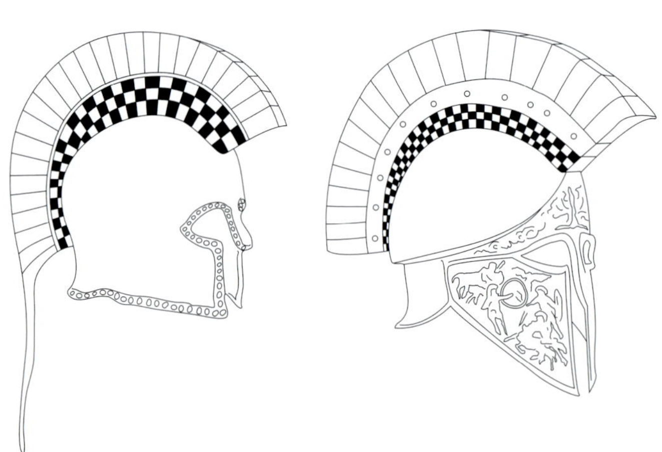

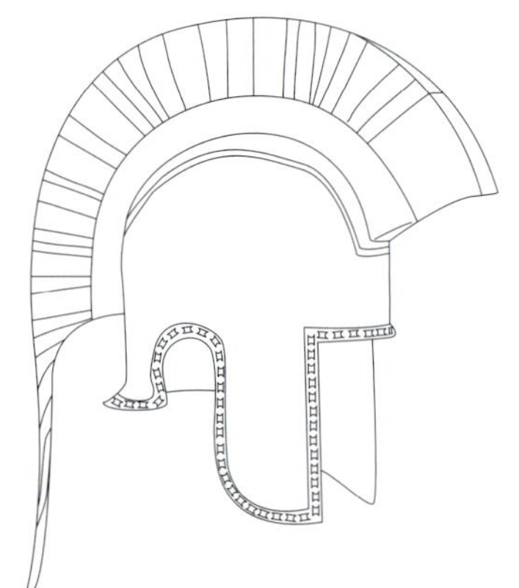

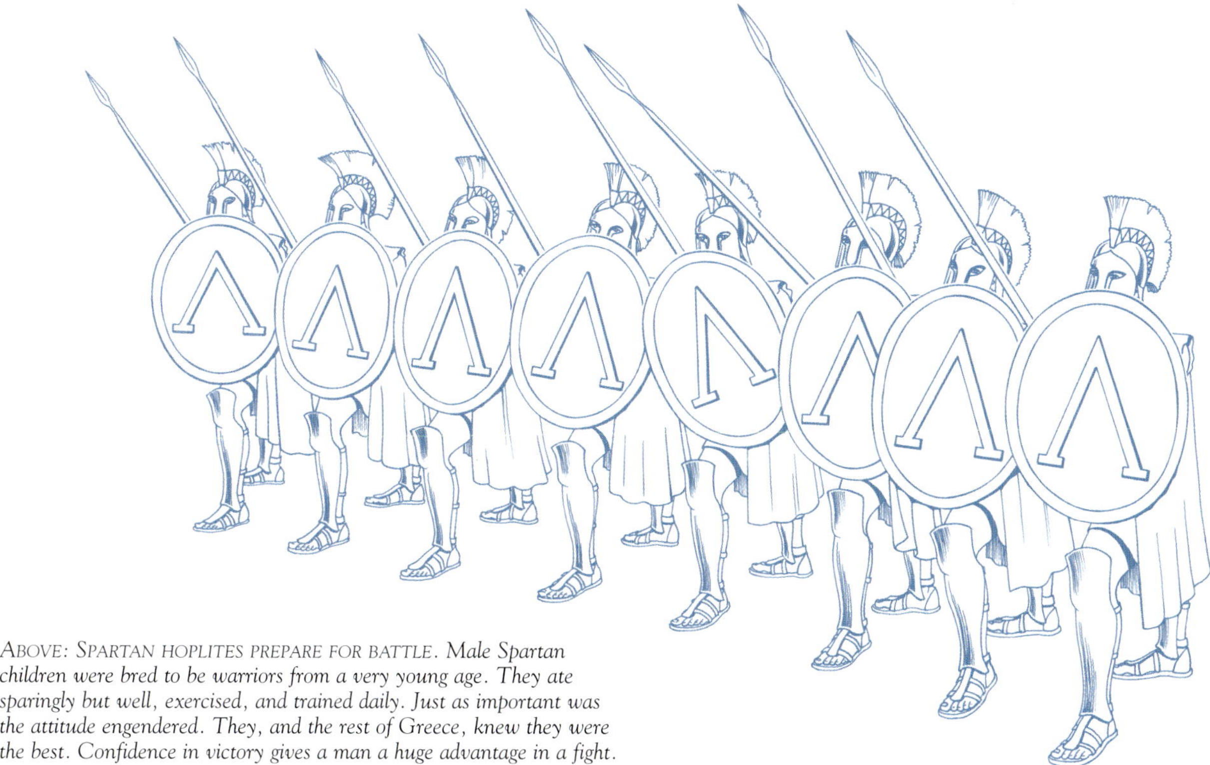

ABOVE: SPARTAN HOPLITES PREPARE FOR BATTLE. Male Spartan children were bred to be warriors from a very young age. They ate sparingly but well, exercised, and trained daily. Just as important was the attitude engendered. They, and the rest of Greece, knew they were the best. Confidence in victory gives a man a huge advantage in a fight.

blockade of the Athenian camp, he advanced to within eight stades, or 1 mile (1.6km), of the Greek positions.

The Greeks advanced from their camp toward the Persian lines. Herodotus recounts that they did so at the run, to reduce the considerable number of arrows that would be shot by the Persians, many of who carried bows. This is very unlikely since to run a mile in heavy hoplite armor would have been nearly impossible and unnecessary—the Athenians likely broke into a jog at about 150 yards (137m)—the range of a Persian bow. The battle lines engaged and the Persians had the better of it in the center where the best of the Persian troops were posted and the Athenians were pushed back. On the wings, however, the levies were routed. Following their orders, the victorious Greeks wheeled in against the Persian center catching them in a double envelopment. A slaughter followed with 6,400 Persian casualties, mostly Iranian and Saka troops, and only 192 Athenians, including Callimachus, and a handful of Plataeans killed. The Greeks also captured seven Persian ships although the others escaped.

AFTERMATH

The Athenians could not, however, rest after their victory. While one tribal division held the field, the remainder made a forced march back to Athens. They arrived in time to deter the Persians from landing and so Datis, now joined by Artaphernes' survivors, was forced to return home. While the Athenians and Plataeans had won a great victory, they had not really won the war.

The Persians returned home where, almost immediately, they undertook preparations for another campaign—although it would take 10 years, the Persians would return in force with any eye to conquering all of Greece, not just punishing the Athenians.

LEFT: POPULAR MYTH HAS IT that following the Greek victory at Marathon, the Athenian runner, Philippides, delivered the news to the worried Athenians 26 miles (42km) away. The modern marathon race celebrates his feat.

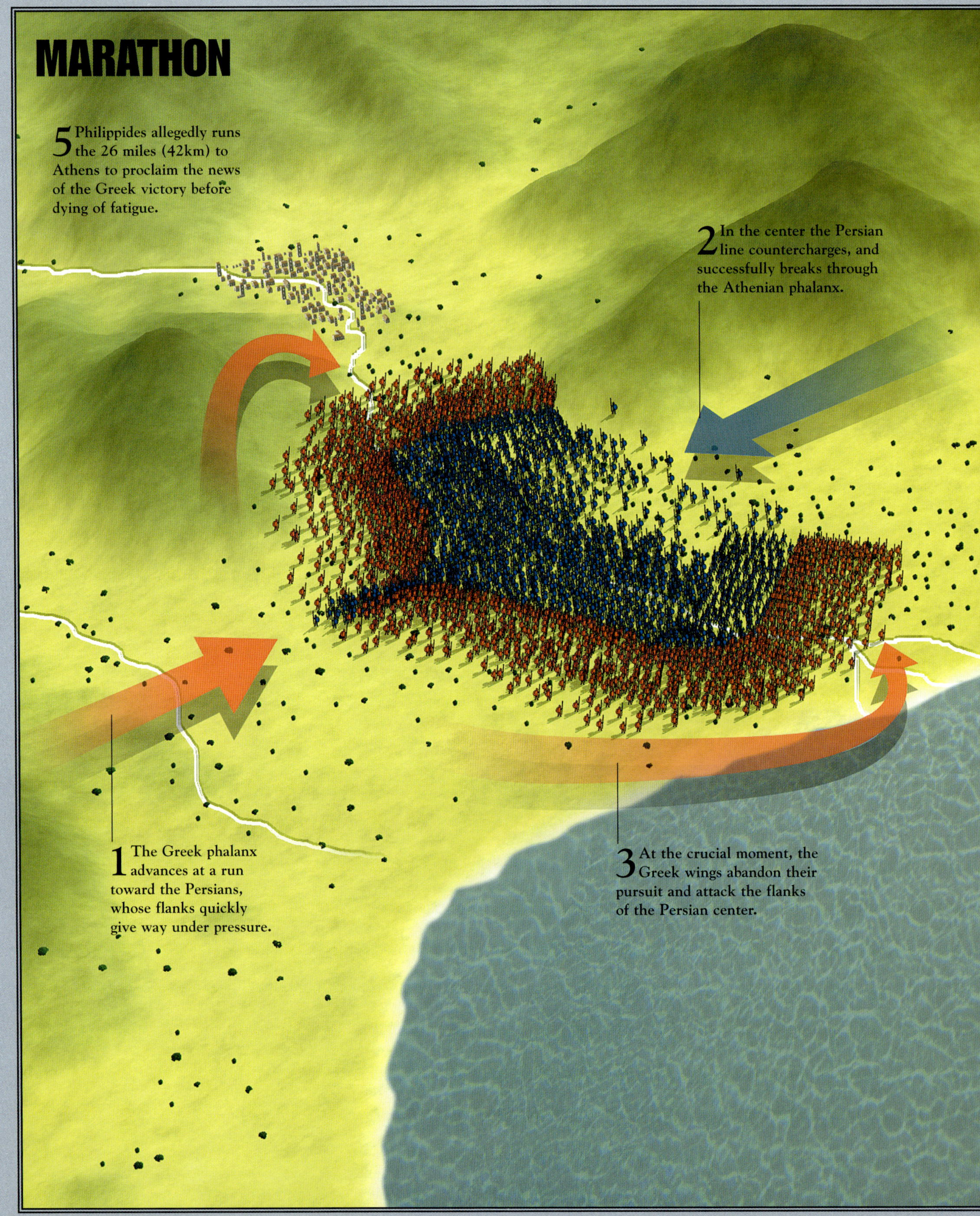
MARATHON
5 Philippides allegedly runs the 26 miles (42km) to Athens to proclaim the news of the Greek victory before dying of fatigue.
2 In the center the Persian line countercharges, and successfully breaks through the Athenian phalanx.
1 The Greek phalanx advances at a run toward the Persians, whose flanks quickly give way under pressure.
3 At the crucial moment, the Greek wings abandon their pursuit and attack the flanks of the Persian center.

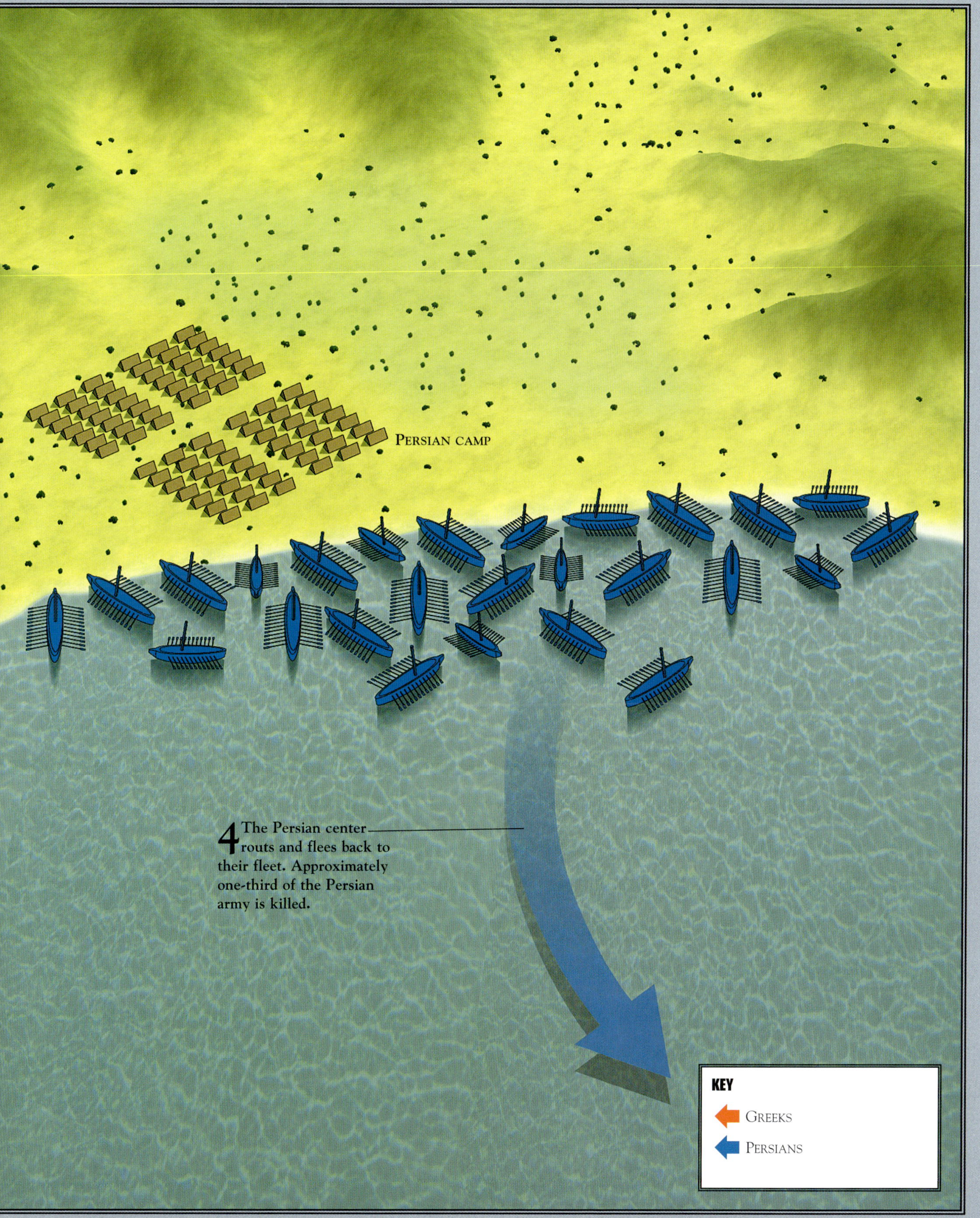

Persian camp
4 The Persian center routs and flees back to their fleet. Approximately one-third of the Persian army is killed.
KEY
Greeks
Persians

ALESIA

52 B.C.E.

Caesar's victory at Alesia, where Roman skill at military engineering enabled him to defeat a vast Gallic army coming to relieve their chieftain Vercingetorix, besieged in the town, secured Roman rule in Gaul. But for all his fortifications, Caesar had a hard fight of it.

In 59 B.C.E., Gaius Julius Caesar was elected consul in Rome. He used his position and political connections to secure his appointment as the governor of Cisalpine and Transalpine Gaul and Illyricum at the conclusion of his consulship. He took up the governorship the following year and used the migration of the Helvetii, and the trepidation this caused among Rome's Gallic allies, as a pretext to intervene militarily in Gaul. While it does not seem that Caesar initially intended to conquer Gaul, his victory over the Helvetii may have provided him with the opportunity to contemplate doing so. Over the next five years Caesar waged a number of successful, if sometimes close-run, campaigns in Gaul, forcing many tribes to submit to him, at least temporarily. Moreover, Caesar also launched campaigns across the Rhine and twice invaded Britain.

ALESIA FACTS

Who: Gaius Julius Caesar (100–44 B.C.E.), with an army of 45,000 men, besieged an army of around 70,000 Gauls under Vercingetorix of the Arverni (d. 46 B.C.E.) and faced a relief force reputed to number 250,000 warriors.

What: Caesar made use of the Roman skill at siege warfare by constructing lines of siege works facing both inward and outward and Roman discipline to defeat threats from both the besieged and relieving forces.

Where: Alesia, some 30 miles (48km) northwest of modern Dijon in France.

When: Late September/early October 52 B.C.E.

Why: Caesar sought to defeat Vercingetorix's threat to Roman rule once and for all.

Outcome: The battle was the last major effort by the Gauls against Caesar. The defeat of the charismatic Vercingetorix and the sizeable forces mustered for the battle ended the Gauls' ability to resist the Romans.

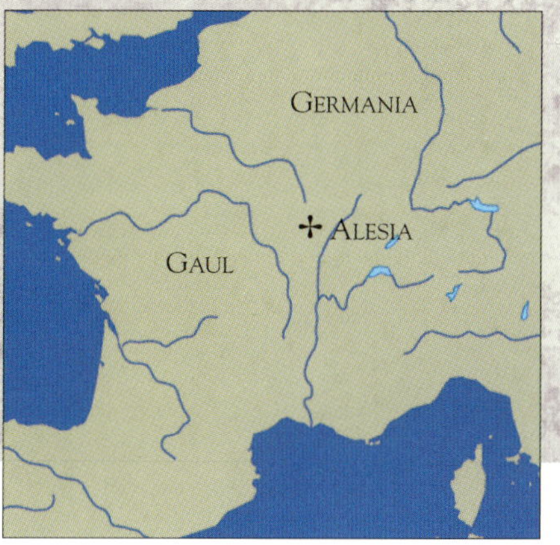

LEFT: LEGIONARIES CONSTRUCT DEFENSIVE WORKS. *The Roman army were unparalleled in the ancient world as builders of small fortresses. They were also highly skilled at building defensive walls.*

Despite his success, there was definite unrest in Gaul which began to manifest itself in late 54 B.C.E. Due to a bad harvest, Caesar was forced to disperse his troops in winter quarters throughout much of northeast Gaul, requiring the various tribes to provide his troops with provisions. This led to serious resentment that burst into open rebellion. Two legionary encampments were attacked during the winter of 54/53 B.C.E. A legion of 10 cohorts with five additional cohorts, perhaps the cadre of a new legion, under the command of Quintus Titurius Sabinus and Lucius Aurunculeius Cotta, was destroyed when the Romans were lured from their fortified camp, ambushed, and annihilated. This was followed by an attack on a legion in winter camp under the command of Quintus Tullius Cicero (the brother of the famous orator Marcus Tullius Cicero). Cicero wisely remained within his fortifications and, although his force was hard-pressed and suffered extraordinarily heavy losses, was able to hold out until he was relieved. Caesar spent the remainder of 53 B.C.E. raising additional forces, intimidating Gallic tribes, and dealing with the Germans, both campaigning across the Rhine and fighting off a major raid.

THE CAMPAIGN AND THE ARMIES

At the beginning of 52 B.C.E., the Gauls planned a coordinated effort that would become a general rebellion aimed at expelling the Romans. The revolt began early in the year with the massacre of Roman citizens living at Cenabum, city-state of the Carnuntes tribe. This signal inspired the Gauls, and a young, charismatic noble of the Arverni, Vercingetorix, to put together a coalition of tribes and put a significant army in the field. The Gauls began by attacking the capital of the Boii, a tribe still allied with Rome, but Caesar, who had been away in Italy, returned and forced the Gauls to withdraw. Meanwhile, Caesar attacked several Gallic towns, no doubt in order to procure supplies at this difficult time of year. Vercingetorix realized that logistics were Caesar's weak point and so the Gauls adopted a Fabian strategy where they would avoid open battle with the Romans and fall back on and defend their fortified towns in an attempt to deny the Romans much-needed supplies.

Meanwhile, Caesar continued to attack Gallic towns and attempted to force a confrontation. He moved into the territory of the Bituriges and attacked their major stronghold, Avaricium. Vercingetorix had tried to convince the Bituriges to abandon the town, but they were confident in its defenses. Though he camped outside the town, he was unable to prevent the Romans from investing the town. Caesar attacked the town in a rainstorm when it was least expected and was able to take it, forcing Vercingetorix to retire. Caesar took six legions and marched on the capital of the Arverni at Gergovia. This town was clearly important to Vercingetorix and he intended to defend it. When Caesar reached the town, which was located in very hilly terrain, he seized a hill and established a fortified camp there. He quickly took another hill, established a small camp there, and connected the two with a pair of parallel ditches. Caesar noticed a small hill, which provided access to the town and was virtually undefended. He ordered some of his troops to

BELOW: A RECONSTRUCTED FORT at modern-day Alesia. The double ditch and abatis (sharp sticks projecting from the wall) were not intended to stop attackers so much as to slow them down so that missile fire from within the fort could kill more of them.

provide a distraction and then launched an attack on the hill, which he took with relative ease. The troops, however, continued on to the town walls, whether at Caesar's direction or, as he would have it, having simply been carried away by their success, where they met stiff resistance and were driven off with heavy losses, particularly among the centurions. At that point, Caesar was forced to raise the siege and withdraw from Gergovia.

The defeat at Gergovia was a serious blow to Caesar and a benefit to Vercingetorix. The defeat caused some of Caesar's oldest Gallic allies to defect to the enemy. Vercingetorix set about recruiting additional troops for the rebellion and, using a large cavalry force, began interdicting Roman efforts to gather supplies. Caesar was not idle. To make up the losses caused by the defections, especially in his cavalry, he recruited German cavalry and light infantry to support them. It became clear to Vercingetorix that his forces could not stand up to Caesar's in open battle, particularly with the addition of the German cavalry, and decided to fall back on the fortified town of Alesia, hoping to repeat the defeat of the Romans at Gergovia. Caesar followed him and prepared to invest the town.

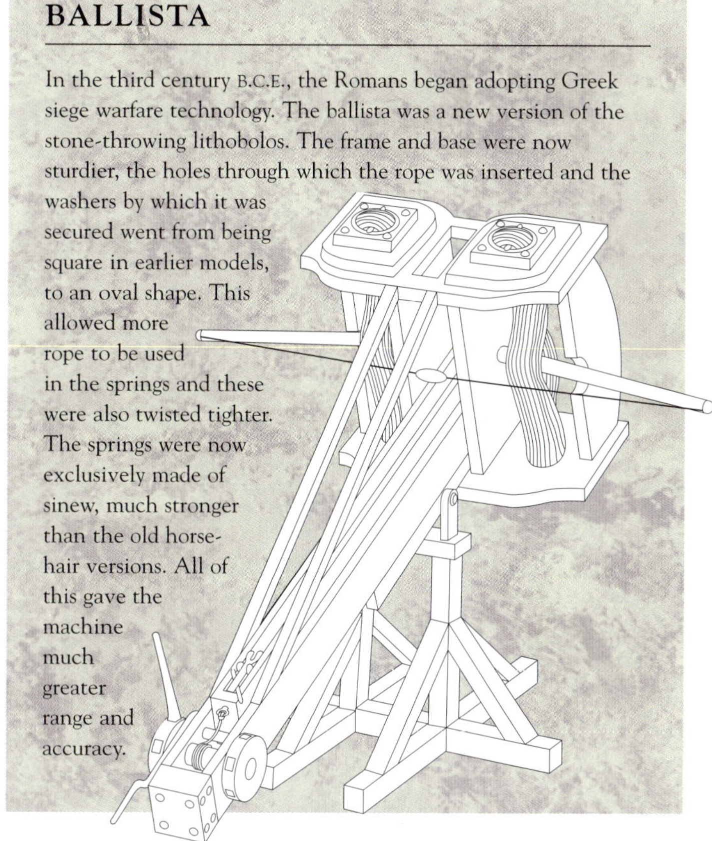

BALLISTA

In the third century B.C.E., the Romans began adopting Greek siege warfare technology. The ballista was a new version of the stone-throwing lithobolos. The frame and base were now sturdier, the holes through which the rope was inserted and the washers by which it was secured went from being square in earlier models, to an oval shape. This allowed more rope to be used in the springs and these were also twisted tighter. The springs were now exclusively made of sinew, much stronger than the old horse-hair versions. All of this gave the machine much greater range and accuracy.

DISPOSITIONS

Vercingetorix and his army built a fortified camp adjacent to Alesia defended by a ditch and rampart, 6ft (1.8m) high. Caesar concluded that Alesia and the Gallic camp were far too strong to be assaulted and so decided instead to surround and blockade the town. He started by constructing seven fortified camps supported by 23 redoubts to defend key positions. While these fortifications were being constructed, Vercingetorix sent out his cavalry to interfere with the Romans. A cavalry battle ensued in which the Gauls were badly mauled by Caesar's cavalry, especially the Germans. Vercingetorix then decided to have his cavalry attempt a breakout during the night. The Gallic horsemen slipped out through gaps in the Roman lines and went back to their communities to raise a new army to relieve the siege.

With the escape of the Gallic cavalry and the likely appearance of a relief army, Caesar decided to augment his siege works. First, he constructed a 20ft (6m) ditch with perpendicular sides to prevent the Gauls in Alesia from interfering with his construction of more complete fortifications. Behind this ditch, two additional ditches were dug, and the inner one filled with water to become a moat. Behind these a rampart 12ft (3.6m) high was erected from dirt excavated from the ditches. This was surmounted with a palisade and protected by sharpened stakes. To further reinforce the rampart, towers were placed along its length at regular intervals. The length of these works was nearly 10 miles (16km).

RIGHT: THE PRIMARY WEAPON of the legionary was his deadly sword, used from behind the protection of his shield. Enemies were softened up before a charge, or their charges were broken up, by massed volleys of pilae, or javelins. The pilum was a "fire" weapon used to weaken the enemy so that the "shock" effect of the legionary assault could more easily shatter his formations and drive him from the field.

During the construction of the fortifications, Vercingetorix made a number of substantial and coordinated sorties from the town, which interfered with construction and made it difficult for Caesar to send out foragers. He therefore added three lines of traps to make enemy attack more difficult. The first consisted of five rows of sharpened tree trunks and stout branches set in trenches, in front of them were pits 3ft (90cm) deep arranged in the fashion of a chessboard, with sharpened stakes set inside, and in front, iron hooks set in wooden blocks were scattered around.

In order to defend against the relief army a similar set of fortifications 17 miles (28km) in length were built facing outward with plenty of room in between for Caesar to move his troops. Caesar also had his men collect a one-month reserve of food and fodder. The Gauls within Alesia recognized that supplies would become short so they sent out of the town all of those who were not able to fight. The non-combatants went to the Roman lines but were turned away by Caesar and so were left to starve in a no-man's land.

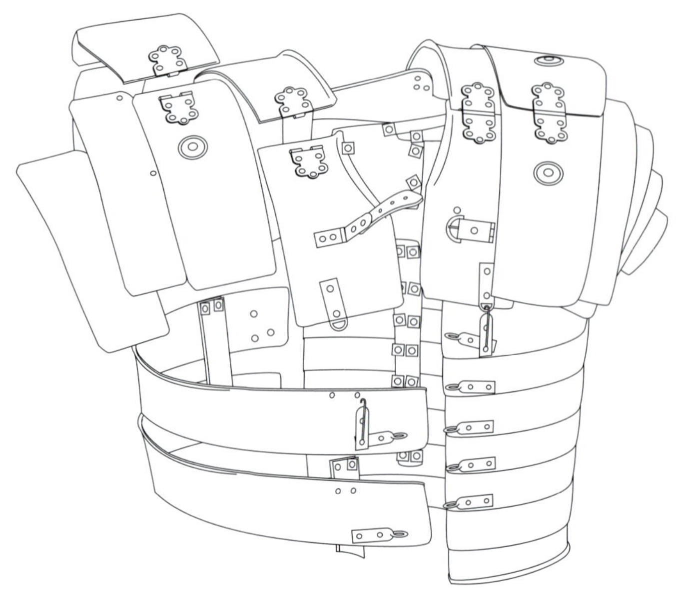

ABOVE: A RECONSTRUCTION OF THE LORICA *segmentata showing how the iron segments are held together with hooks and riveted leather straps to produce a flexible yet effective armor.*

THE BATTLE

The battle began as the relief force arrived and, after having camped within a mile of the Roman lines, sent out their cavalry into a plain 3 miles (4.8km) wide. The Gallic horse had archers and light infantry interspersed, while the main body of infantry formed up to watch their cavalry who were the elite of the army. When the Gauls within Alesia saw the cavalry formed for battle, they came out of the town and started to fill in the Roman trenches with fascines in preparation for a sortie. Caesar responded by manning the ramparts with all of his infantry, making sure each man knew

BELOW: "VERCINGETORIX THROWING HIS WEAPONS AT THE FEET OF CÈSAR," *Lionel-Noël Royer's (1852–1926) depiction of Vercingetorix offers a romanticized view of the Gallic leader's surrender. Caesar is depicted dressed as a political figure rather than a soldier.*

his post, and sending out his Gallic allied and German horse to meet the enemy cavalry. The cavalry action was fiercely contested, the Gallic horse benefiting from the support of the infantry in their midst, something the Romans had not expected. The fighting lasted from noon until sunset, but eventually the Romans had the better of it when Caesar massed his German cavalry at a single point and they broke the Gallic cavalry. The latter fled leaving their infantry supports to be slaughtered and were pursued back to their camp. The Gauls within the siegeworks despaired and retired back to Alesia.

The Gauls of the relief force spent the following day preparing the materials needed for a major assault, including ladders, grappling hooks, and fascines. At midnight, they quietly advanced and, once near the Roman siegeworks, gave a shout to let the besieged know they were beginning the assault. As a result Vercingetorix led out his forces to attack the Romans at the same time so the Romans would be engaged to front and rear. Although the Gauls were able to cause a number of casualties by hurling javelins, slinging stones, and others missiles, the obstacles set up by the Romans before their ramparts made it extremely difficult and caused heavy losses. The Gauls were unable to penetrate the Roman lines and, fearing a counterattack, therefore retreated.

GALLIC WARRIOR

The archetypal barbarian warrior with bare chest, fierce mustache, and patterned pants. The Gallic tribesman was a dangerous foe. Roman writers such as Tacitus praised their courage and stoicism. Gauls had defeated Roman armies on previous occasions, but their main weakness was a lack of good organization. Where the Roman army was a well-drilled and obedient body of professional troops, the Gallic force facing it was a loose collection of proud and aggressive men bound together by ties of personal, tribal, and family loyalties. In a short campaign or while they were winning this was not a problem, but once supplies became an issue and victory was doubtful there was a tendency for Gallic armies to break up and groups to begin to drift away.

The Gauls held a council of war and decided to use the main army to threaten the siegeworks while a force of 60,000 picked men attacked a Roman camp on the north side of the town. This fort was defended by two legions, but due to the nature of the terrain, it lay outside of the lines of circumvallation. Meanwhile Vercingetorix would again lead an attack so the Romans would be forced to defend both the inner and outer defenses against simultaneous assaults. The Gallic force of warriors marched through the night and rested until noon at which point they attacked. At the same time Vercingetorix attacked the inward-facing fortifications so the Romans were hard-pressed at several places. Caesar noticed that the 60,000 Gauls were having some success against the isolated fort and so he sent his most trusted lieutenant, Titus Atius Labienus, to its relief with six cohorts. He ordered Labienus to defend the fort but if it appeared he could no longer defend it, he should instead counterattack. In the meantime, Vercingetorix's troops had breached a steep section of the inner wall where the fortifications were not as complete.

Caesar sent reinforcements to this position, eventually repulsing the Gauls when he personally led some troops to the breach. By this point the situation had become desperate and Labienus was preparing for a last-ditch counterattack. Caesar rushed to aid the counterattack leading a mere four cohorts, but he also ordered his cavalry to sally out and assault the Gallic warriors from behind. Although the Gauls put up a fight, the appearance of cavalry behind them was too much and they were routed. The Roman cavalry were able to cause tremendous casualties among the routing Gauls. The besieged Gauls were dismayed by this turn of events and retired into Alesia.

AFTERMATH

With the rout of the relief army, the Gauls within Alesia were forced to surrender. Vercingetorix was handed over to Caesar. Some of the Gauls were used to help gain the loyalty of their tribes but many were distributed to the troops as booty and ended up as slaves. The victory at Alesia effectively broke Gallic resistance, although Caesar would spend the next two years consolidating his position. Vercingetorix would remain a prisoner for some six years until, after having been paraded in Rome during Caesar's great triumph, he was publicly strangled.

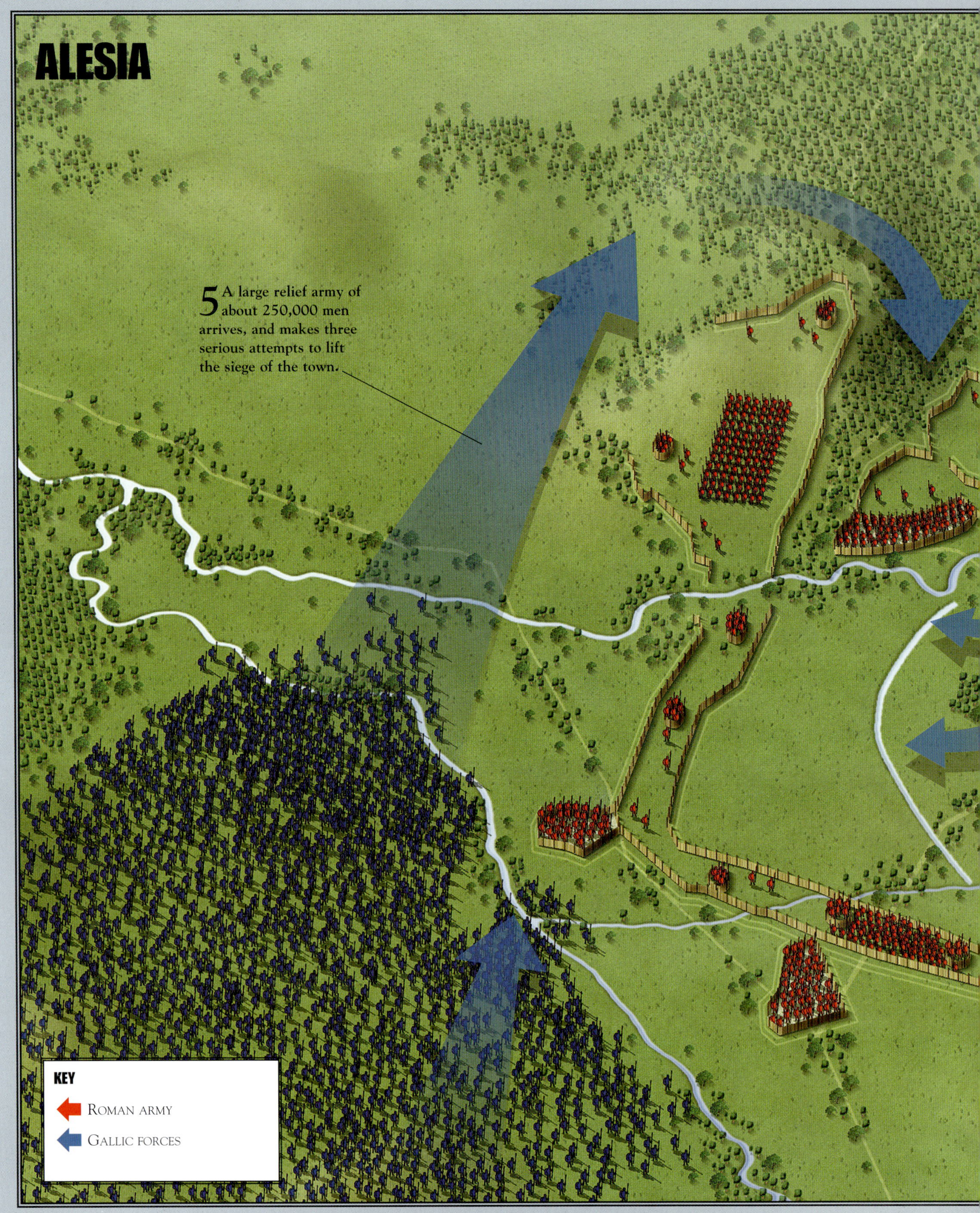
ALESIA
5 A large relief army of about 250,000 men arrives, and makes three serious attempts to lift the siege of the town.
KEY
Roman army
Gallic forces

6 The men inside Alesia coordinate their attacks with the relief army, but are defeated by Caesar's Germanic cavalry.
1 Vercingetorix and approximately 70,000 soldiers take refuge in the fortified hilltop town of Alesia.
4 The women and children are forced out of Alesia to save food, and have to camp between the two forces.
2 After the Gallic cavalry escapes, Caesar builds inner and outer walls of approximately 17.4 miles (28km) in length.
3 Forts are constructed along the walls with plenty of space between them to move troops to trouble spots.

HASTINGS 1066

Norman mounted men-at-arms met the Anglo-Saxon shield wall in the longest, hardest fought, and most decisive battle in England in the early Middle Ages. William the Conqueror's victory changed English history forever, and ushered in the dominance of the mounted knight in European warfare.

In traditional accounts Harold's reputation was blackened as an oath-breaker, while others viewed William as the villain. It is probably safe to say that both of these remarkably able and ruthless men had their good and bad sides. William was the illegitimate son of the Duke of Normandy and he had to defend his position as Duke, from 1035 onward, against all comers and by the time he wished to invade England had carved out the most powerful duchy in France and northwestern Europe, reducing both Brittany and Maine to vassal states. His influence was also predominant in Paris, where he dominated the young King Philip, and he had created a crucial ally in Flanders by marrying Matilda, the daughter of Duke Baldwin IV.

HASTINGS FACTS

Who: William, Duke of Normandy (1028–87), invaded England with an army of 6,000 men to lay claim to the throne of King Harold II Godwinson (1022–66), who faced him with an army of 6,300.

What: Norman cavalry and archers eventually wore down the Saxon shield wall formation.

Where: Senlac Ridge, 7 miles (11.2km) north of the town of Hastings, England.

When: October 14, 1066.

Why: William wanted to conquer England.

Outcome: Harold and most of the Anglo-Saxon nobility were killed, and William secured the throne of England.

LEFT: THIS DRAMATIC DEPICTION of the battle of Hastings by R. Caton Woodville shows King Harold Godwinson making his final stand against the Normans on Senlac Hill.

ABOVE: THE NORMAN ARMY AS DISPLAYED IN THE BAYEUX TAPESTRY consists of cavalry and archers. Other contemporary sources indicate that the cavalry greatly outnumbered the archers, but the latter's role in the death of King Harold Godwinson no doubt accounts for their exaggerated presence.

William's claim to the English throne was very tenuous and lacked solid legal foundations. William had forced his rival, Harold Godwinson, in 1064 to swear an oath to leave Edward the Confessor's throne to him. But Harold had no intention of honoring an oath forced upon him through blackmail and threats. As the Earl of Wessex, vice-regent under Edward since 1064, the elderly King's brother-in-law, and with undoubted ability and good character, no man had a stronger or more legitimate claim to the throne of England. As a consequence when Edward died, on January 5, 1066, Harold was crowned in Westminster Abbey.

STAMFORD BRIDGE

Harold was no fool and he knew that the ruthlessly ambitious William would use his "breaking" of the "oath" as a spurious excuse to invade. Until May there was no threat of invasion but during the early summer William unleashed an ambitious naval building program to create an armada of 500 ships to carry his 6,000-strong army (of Normans, Bretons, French, and Flemings) across the Channel.

In response Harold mobilized his 4,000-strong Royal Guard, known by their Scandinavian name of huscarls, and the territorial Saxon militia, the fyrd. The fyrd could, in theory and given time, resources, and money, mobilize 15,000–20,000 men but during the summer of 1066 it probably numbered no more than 4,000. Harold strung out his army of 8,000 men along the south coast waiting for the Normans. Harold ordered the fyrd to be disbanded on September 8 so these men could return to their farms and gather in the all-important harvest. Unfortunately Harold had acted precipitously because news arrived that his brother, Earl Tostig, had joined forces with King Harald Hardrada of Norway and had invaded northern England. As Harold gathered his men and rushed north, the Saxon army of the north, led by the Earl of Northumbria, were defeated on September 20 at Fulford Gate. Five days later Harold surprised and annihilated the Norwegian invaders, slaying Tostig and Harald in the process, at Stamford Bridge.

WILLIAM'S INVASION

Back in France, William had been kept in Normandy by contrary winds. It was only on September 12 that his armada could sail to St. Valéry on the Somme River from where he intended to invade England. It was only a short day's sailing across the Channel to England from this small port. The winds proved fickle and it was not until September 27 that a southerly wind allowed William's fleet to set sail northward. He made landfall at Pevensey Bay the following morning and immediately started gathering supplies, erecting his wooden forts (portable ones brought from Normandy in sections), and plundering the surrounding countryside for intelligence, food, and fodder for his horses.

News that William had finally landed reached Harold at York on October 1 amid celebrations following Stamford Bridge. Harold rushed south picking up the fyrd and other troops along the way back to London. He left the capital on October 11 heading south with an army of 6,000–7,000 troops. Many of his men rode to the battle on horses but would fight on foot. It was late in the afternoon on October 13 that Harold reached Senlac Ridge, a location that he had, during the summer's idleness, chosen as a possible battleground. His choice was based on his experience fighting the Welsh (1064) and his familiarity with the Hastings region.

Senlac was a gently sloped ridge with a marsh area to the south around the Asten brook with its western and eastern flanks protected by deep ravines covered by thick brushwood. An even steeper ridge protected the northern side and would thus prevent the Normans from attacking Harold's army in the rear. William was rapidly informed about Harold's movement and the arrival of his army. Because the Saxons had arrived late in the day they would opt to rest and then make a lightning attack in the morning. But William would himself make the first move. His men were roused little after five in the morning and by 6 A.M. the Normans were marching northward to face Harold's host. Before they set off William spoke to them telling them, "You fight not merely for victory but also for survival."

William's claim may seem melodramatic but it was the naked truth: if they failed to defeat the Saxons on hostile English soil then they would probably not escape home to Normandy alive. William divided his army into three divisions that marched off with the Bretons as the vanguard, followed by the Franco-Flemish troops and then finally William leading his own Normans. William had chosen as the assembly point the Blackhorse Hill, on the Hastings to London road, where the Bretons arrived by 7:30 A.M. Here, out of sight of the Saxons, William left his baggage train and ordered his men to put on their chain-mail hauberk armor which they had slung across the back of their horses. Unfortunately William put his hauberk on back-to-front, viewed by his superstitious men as a bad omen, but one that the cynical William simply laughed off. The Norman army marched north to take up position opposite the Saxons.

NORMAN KNIGHT

During the eleventh century, Norman horsemen dominated five military theatres: England, northern France, southern Italy, Sicily, and the Holy Land. Their body armor, called a hauberk by this time, was mail and made in one piece. Most hauberks reached to the knees and were divided down the front and back by slits that allowed greater freedom of movement and comfort. Other defensive equipment included the kite shield and helmet. A long lance was the chief weapon of the Norman horseman, while a sword could be used for close combat.

DISPOSITIONS

William remained on a small knoll out of the way under the Papal banner and his own Norman leopard standards. From this position he could give orders and had a good view of the battlefield. He could observe how the Bretons under Count Alan of Brittany followed the Asten brook to take up position opposite Harold's right flank. On William's left, Count Eustace of Boulogne led his French and Flemish mercenaries to the bottom of Senlac Ridge facing the Saxon left. In the middle now stood the largest and most formidable of the divisions: William's own Normans with auxiliaries from Anjou and Main. The archers and crossbowmen were at the front, then came the more heavily armed infantry and finally William's mounted men-at-arms.

For his part, Harold had been aware that the invaders were on the move since 8 A.M. when his scouts reported that the Normans had left Blackhorse Hill. If the weather had been wetter, forcing William to postpone his attack for a few crucial hours, Harold might have had time to erect proper defenses atop Senlac Ridge but there was no rain and the ground was firm. Harold's army was roused and began to deploy along the ridge in a shield wall that stretched for 600 yards (549m) from the Asten brook to the junction of the roads to Hastings and Seddlescombe. The Saxon phalanx was 10 ranks deep with 2ft (0.6m) of frontage for each of his warriors meaning that he had about 6,300 men under his command. William had placed his strongest division in the center so Harold followed suit, placing his more experienced

Right: English shield wall, mid-eleventh century. The troops are mainly spearmen, though some hold axes and swords. The formation depended on the mutual support of the men within it for its strength.

RIGHT: A ROMANTIC PORTRAYAL of William the Conqueror from a nineteenth-century illustration. Born an illegitimate son of the Duke Robert of Normandy, he became one of the greatest military leaders in history, fighting off rebels in his own duchy and conquering Maine, parts of Brittany, and England.

huscarls in the center. He placed his lighter armed and armored men of the fyrd on the flanks, reinforced by a line of sharpened wooden stakes in front.

THE BATTLE BEGINS

October 14, the Feast of St. Calixtus, dawned with brightening skies, a thin cloud cover and no indication of rain. Aged 44, Harold faced the 38-year-old William. They were both gifted and experienced commanders in their prime leading two of the best armies in western Europe, whose morale was superb: the Normans because of the prospect of conquest and loot; the Saxons because of the need to defend their homeland and their recent spectacular victory at Stamford Bridge. The Normans, who would have to make the first move, were 150 yards (137m) from, and 50ft (15.24m) below, the Saxon shield wall. The Bretons were the least experienced of William's troops and the weak link in his army. Harold's equivalent were the fyrd and he trusted his shield wall to hold back the onrush of Norman cavalry—it was the first time a predominantly cavalry army was fighting infantry in this fashion. The outcome would decide the nature of medieval warfare thereafter.

Sharp trumpet blasts at 9 A.M. announced the beginning of the battle as William's three divisions advanced up the slope of Senlac Ridge. The archers at the front showered the Saxons with arrows but to little effect—these either overshot their intended target or got lodged in the shield wall. The Saxon response with javelins, spears, and axes proved far more effective against the onrushing Normans. Because they had the gentler slope, the jittery Bretons were the first to smash into the shield wall and be repelled by the fierce resistance of the Saxons. Unnerved by this and the failure of the archers' fire to make any impact on the shield wall, the Bretons retreated by 10–10:30 A.M. The retreat turned into a rout when the undisciplined fyrd militia left the safety of the shield wall to pursue the fleeing Bretons.

WILLIAM'S ATTACK

From his vantage point, William saw what was happening and with a curse he gathered part of the advancing Norman cavalry to assist the hard-pressed Bretons. Riding into the fyrd with a charge of armored knights, the Saxons were taken by surprise and, as lightly armored infantry on open ground, they were cut down to the last man. William's timely and ferocious cavalry charge had saved his army from disaster. Undoubtedly morale, especially among the defeated Bretons, was low. William recalled his other two divisions, halted for half an hour to regroup for another attack. This time the advance would be slower and more deliberate with the cavalry at the

RIGHT: THE MOST FEARSOME military tactic of the Middle Ages was the cavalry charge, as demonstrated here by Norman horse. At a time when success in battle often depended more on forcing one's enemies to flee the battlefield than on actually killing them, resisting such a charge depended on the discipline of lower-class infantry troops.

helm supported by archers and infantry following behind. William, taking personal charge, began the second attack at 11:00 A.M. The ground was slippery from the previous attack and littered with dead men and horses, so progress was slow and hesitant.

Waves of attacks were launched against the shield wall for two hours. The Normans managed to make a few, small holes in the line but Harold and his commanders, including his brothers Gyrth (Earl of East Anglia) and Leofwine (Earl of Kent), steadied their men, plugged the gaps, and showered the enemy with missiles. Harold's Fighting Man standard and the Dragon Pennant of Wessex had been placed at the center of the Saxon lines to encourage the defenders.

NEAR ROUT

Finally, by 1 P.M., even the tough Flemish and French troops had had enough; they broke and began to flee from the ridge. Their commander Eustace grabbed the Papal standard, rallied his fleeing men, and admonished them to return to the fight. William had already lost his Spanish charger and was fighting on foot when a rumor reached him that he was dead. Eustace gave the Duke a horse to mount and show himself to his men. William tore off his helmet so that his troops could recognize him and shouted: "Look at me well. I am still alive and by the grace of God shall yet prove victor!" In reality William was losing the battle and he stared defeat in the face. Had the Saxons held their line indefinitely then he would have been forced to retreat back to Hastings and return across the Channel.

At 2 P.M. William called his men and returned them to his own lines below the ridge to regroup, rest, and feed his hungry men. Harold used this respite to shorten his thinning line since Saxon losses, whatever the Normans may have thought, had been considerable and Harold was worried that he would run out of men to plug the ever-rising number of holes in the line. But at least his men were more rested than the Normans who faced an ever more debris-ridden and cluttered slope as they prepared for a renewed attack.

Having lost one-quarter of his army, or around 1,800–1,900 men, in five hours of almost continuous fighting, as well as a horrendous number of horses, cut down by the axe-wielding Saxons, William saw that many of his men-at-arms were now fighting on foot. He decided that the whole army would attack in a single formation of all arms combined.

The third and final attack saw the entire army advance with archers at the back, from around 3 P.M., at a slow pace. It took the Normans an agonizing half-hour to reach the Saxon line. William had ordered the archers to shoot as high as possible while the infantry, dismounted knights, and still-mounted cavalry gave their utmost in attacking the shield wall. Finally the shield wall began to waver, break in places and then come apart under the Norman onslaught. Once a hole had been created in the wall the Norman cavalry poured through and, with their lances, sword, and spears, tore at the soft underbelly of the Saxon army. After 4 P.M. the breach became unstoppable and the fighting degenerated into group actions and hand-to-hand combat. This fighting went on until 5:30 P.M. with undiminished ferocity as men fought for their lives. Then the fyrd began to retreat, fleeing into the woods while the huscarls fought on until they were overwhelmed and killed. A large group rallied around Harold's standard as William joined his men on the ridge and had his third and final horse killed under him. Harold led his men with customary tenacity and courage, setting a personal example for his huscarls. But there were not enough of them to fight back the Normans. Gyrth and Leofwin, leading their own huscarls, were killed.

The final straw was the death of Harold himself. He was cut down by the Normans leading his few remaining huscarls. As darkness closed in on the battlefield, small groups of Saxons continued fighting until they could slip away into the surrounding countryside. They rallied and ambushed the pursuing Normans at Oakwood Gill, a small stream north of Senlac Ridge, and managed to cut down Eustace of Boulogne. That was small consolation for the death of Harold.

AFTERMATH

Both sides had lost more than 2,000 men, the Normans well over one-third of their army. For William, it was a triumph against the odds that led to him being crowned as king of England on December 25, 1066. The Saxons would continue to resist their Norman invader for decades after their defeat at Hastings, but were eventually defeated.

SAXON HUSCARL

The Huscarls were an oath-sworn bodyguard of the Anglo-Danish aristocracy, which ruled England prior to the Norman Conquest of 1066. This man wields a long-handled axe, which could decapitate a horse. He has slung his kite-shaped shield on his back to allow him a double-handed grip for extra weight in the blow.

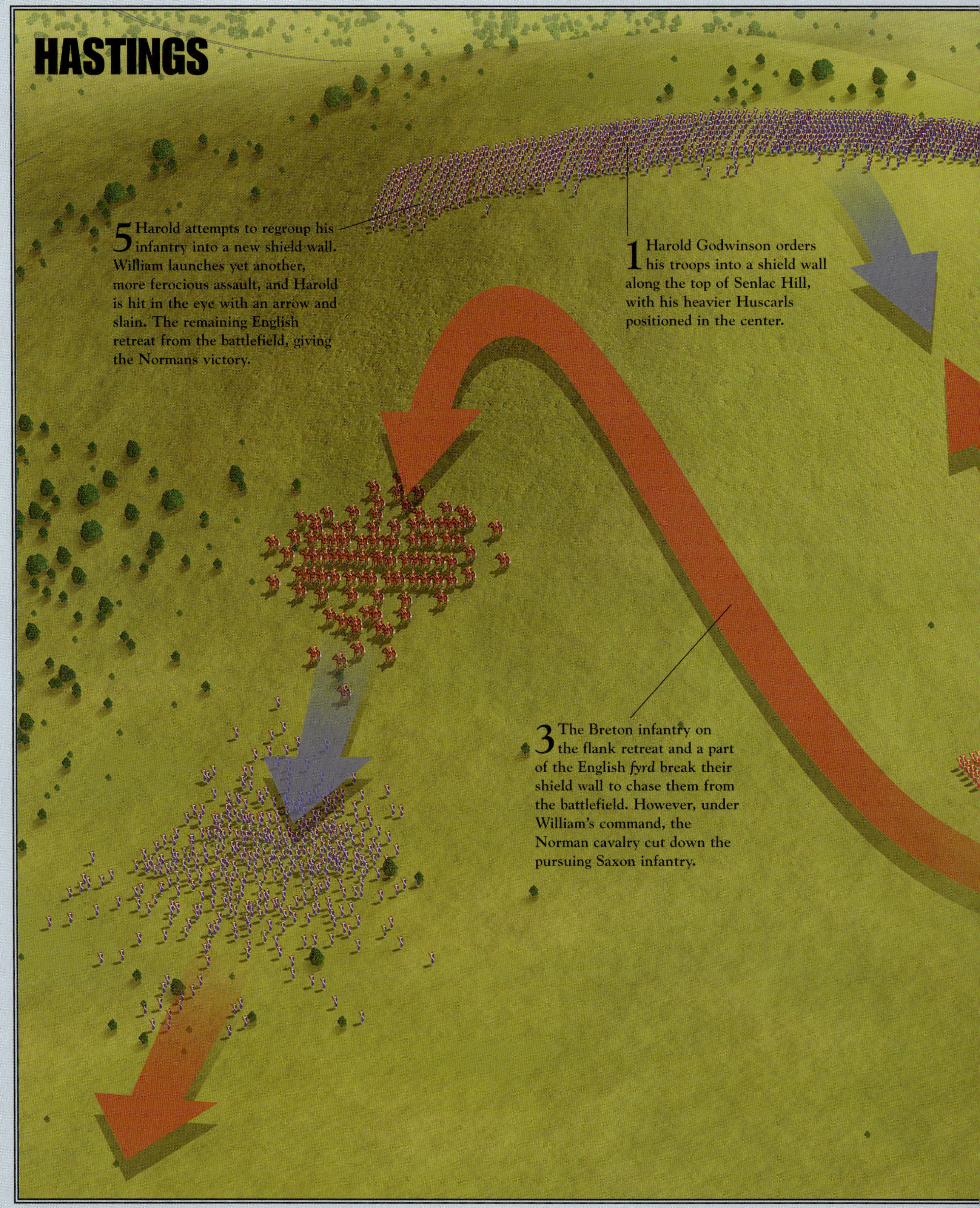
HASTINGS
5 Harold attempts to regroup his infantry into a new shield wall. William launches yet another, more ferocious assault, and Harold is hit in the eye with an arrow and slain. The remaining English retreat from the battlefield, giving the Normans victory.
1 Harold Godwinson orders his troops into a shield wall along the top of Senlac Hill, with his heavier Huscarls positioned in the center.
3 The Breton infantry on the flank retreat and a part of the English *fyrd* break their shield wall to chase them from the battlefield. However, under William's command, the Norman cavalry cut down the pursuing Saxon infantry.

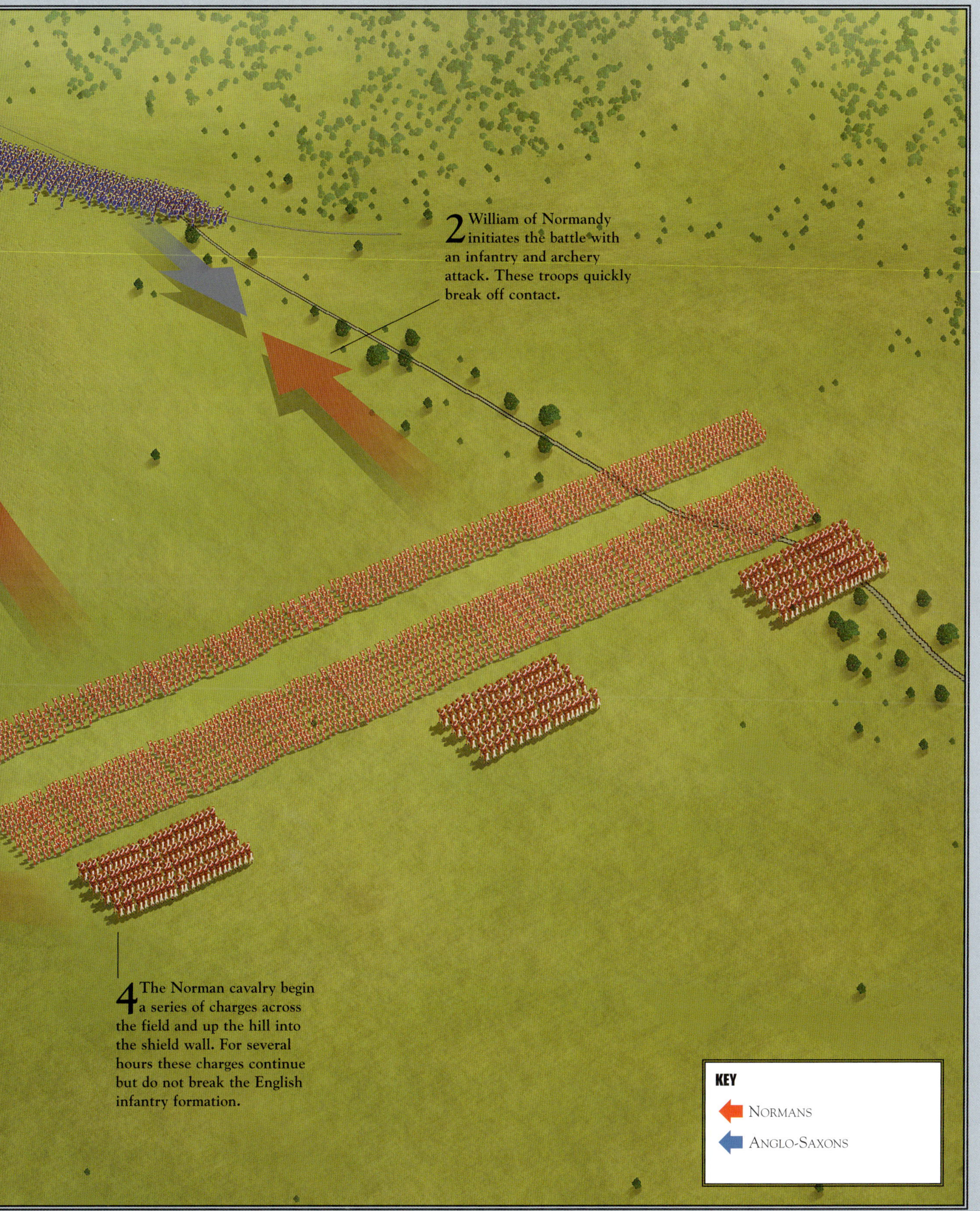
2 William of Normandy initiates the battle with an infantry and archery attack. These troops quickly break off contact.
4 The Norman cavalry begin a series of charges across the field and up the hill into the shield wall. For several hours these charges continue but do not break the English infantry formation.
KEY
Normans
Anglo-Saxons

TANNENBERG 1410

The decisive battle of Tannenberg, between the army of the Teutonic Knights and the Royal Army of Poland-Lithuania, brought to a halt the eastward expansion of the hitherto invincible military order and secured the independence of Poland-Lithuania.

Founded in Acre in 1190 to defend the Holy Land, the Teutonic Order was a military order of warrior-monks whose military and religious reputation could be equated with the Knights of St. John or the Templars. But unlike their rivals the Teutonic Order moved the seat of their activities and crusades to the southern and eastern coasts of the Baltic. The neighboring Poles, whose once united kingdom by this time had become divided into independent duchies, were under constant attack from these hostile pagans, although the Lithuanians, who had carved out a huge realm by conquering Mongol-occupied western Russia, had eventually become Christian and allies of the Poles.

But that still left the marauding and savage Prusy to be dealt with. Lacking resources or the willpower to deal with them, Prince Conrad of Mazovia, whose duchy

TANNENBERG FACTS

Who: The army of the Teutonic Order under their Grand Master Ulrich von Jungingen (d. 1410) fought the Royal Army of Poland-Lithuania under King Wladislaw II Jagiello (1350–1434).

What: The Royal Army of Poland-Lithuania, with Tartar (Mongol) and Russian auxiliaries, annihilated the more experienced and heavily armed Teutonic army.

Where: On a shallow grass plain between the East Prussian (Mazurian) villages of Tannenberg and Grünwald.

When: July 15, 1410.

Why: The Royal Army were caught by surprise when the whole Teutonic army bore down on them before they were prepared but the Teutons squandered a great opportunity to secure a victory by not attacking first.

Outcome: The Polish-Lithuanian victory halted the Teutonic Order's eastward expansion and effectively broke its power.

LEFT: THIS PAINTING BY POLISH MILITARY ARTIST Wojciech von Kossak (1824–99) gives a taste of the bloody battle, with the Royal army in close combat with the Teutons—the screams of wounded men, the neighing of horses, the clank of armor; dust, heat, and sudden death.

was most exposed to Prusy attacks, in 1230 invited the Teutonic Order to crush the Prusy. The Order was only too glad to oblige and a decade later the Prusy threat had been eliminated leaving only pockets of resistance. Conrad quickly regretted ever having invited these rapacious and acquisitive Germans into territories that Poland viewed as vassal states.

EASTWARD EXPANSION

By 1283 the Order controlled both western and eastern Pruthenia or Prussia including the vitally important seaport city of Danzig (now Gdansk)—Poland's only port and point of contact with the West. As if this was not bad enough the Teutonic Order merged with the Order of the Sword Brethren—it too composed of German warrior-monks—that had conquered the Baltic states including the great seaport of Riga. The Order was now the dominant military and political power in the region and a growing threat to its neighbors especially because its huge state was backed by the region's best army and cavalry force. The Poles, Lithuanians, and the Novgorod Russians were equally threatened by the Order. Through a victory over the Sword Brethren in 1242 at Lake Peipus, Novgorod had been saved. It was Poland's turn next. The Order, meanwhile, had not only conquered Prussia but during the period 1310–50 encouraged German colonists to establish 1,400 villages in the territory. Clearly the Order intended not only to conquer but colonize Poland and Lithuania as well, despite both nations being loyal Christians.

In the face of an overwhelming threat Poland was finally, in 1320, reunited under King Wladislaw I (1320–33). Civil war and chaos threatened when he left no male heirs, Poland being ruled by his daughter Queen Jadwiga. She, however, proved a shrewd and able ruler in her own right and she offered her hand in marriage—in order to unite Poland and Lithuania—to the much older Lithuanian Grand Duke Jagiello (1350–1434) who had only recently been christened, appropriately enough, Wladislaw.

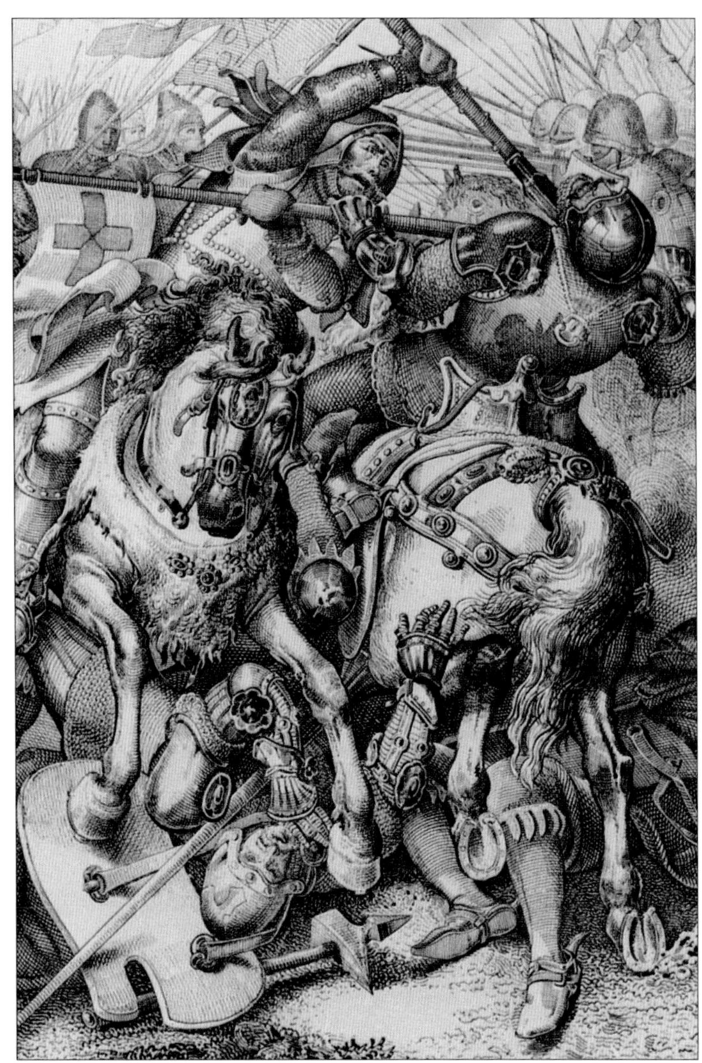

ABOVE: THIS DRAMATIC BATTLE SCENE shows Grand Duke Jagiello supposedly tearing the standard from a Teutonic Knight, signaling the order's defeat.

ABOVE: LITHUANIAN INFANTRYMEN of the fifteenth century were armed in a variety of ways, including long-handled axes (as here), conical, Norse-style helmets, and chainmail. This was a consequence of Lithuania's geography, which reflected a mixture of Nordic and Russian military influences.

Poland had acquired a powerful ally in their quest to crush the Order and regain control over Danzig and Prussia. Lithuania had a formidable army in its own right, which had defeated the Mongols and emulated their superlative tactics, equipment and horsemanship of the steppes' lightning war. In 1386 Jadwiga married Jagiello and the Royal Commonwealth of Poland-Lithuania was founded. When the Order sought to wrest the Lithuanian province of Samogitia from the Grand Duke, Poland was ruled by Jagiello. War was now inevitable but shrewdly Jagiello wanted his enemy to make the first move.

THE OPPOSING ARMIES

Fighting, let alone defeating the Order, was no easy proposition for Jagiello since the Order's army had been victorious ever since its appearance in the region in 1230. Its heavy cavalry of men-at-arms clad in white surcoats with black crosses, numbering some 2,000–3,000 men, were probably the best in Europe and formed the superlative core of an outstanding military machine. Superbly disciplined, mounted, equipped, trained, and experienced, the Teutonic Knights had no equals in Europe let alone the east Baltic region. But with the technological progress of the fourteenth century, the Order had to supplement its knights with mercenaries and specialists such as English longbowmen, Genoese crossbowmen, German and Swiss infantry, and French artillery. All in all the army of the Order was a dangerous and formidable foe.

By contrast the Poles and Lithuanians were far weaker and with less reason to be confident of a victory if faced with the grim-faced German warrior-monks. The Poles had a conventional European-style medieval army of no particular distinction or reputation as yet. As in France the Polish infantry was made up of reluctant, poorly disciplined and motivated peasant conscripts who would rather be working on their farms than fighting their proud and uncaring Lord's wars. In the face of the superior Teutonic infantry they would either fight with customary Polish bravery or, if the mood took them, simply run away at the first enemy charge. The cavalry, mainly composed of Poland's proud and insanely brave nobility, were well mounted, equipped, and motivated. While they were more than a match, man-for-man, to the Teutons, they lacked the warrior-monks' experience and discipline.

ABOVE: MEDIEVAL ARMOR SUITS were most often made of chain links or metal scales. Chain armor (favored in Western Europe) consisted of thousands of round metal rings, the ring ends welded or riveted together. Scale armor (favored in Eastern Europe and Byzantium) was made of a large number of metallic scales attached to each other by wire or leather laces.

By contrast the Lithuanian host was more Asiatic than European in appearance, equipment, and tactics because they had fought for centuries against the Mongol occupiers of Russia. As a consequence they placed great reliance upon skirmishing, maneuvering, and mobility with light and medium cavalry forces rather than a head-on collision with heavy cavalry and massed infantry. If these warriors faced the

BELOW: IN THIS PAINTING by Jan Matejko (1838–93), the Polish-Lithuanian army is at the point of crushing the reeling and bleeding troops of the Order, with a triumphant Jagiello in the center of the action.

TEUTONIC KNIGHT

The roots of the Teutonic Order were military-monastic in the simple white garb with its equally simple cross as the only decoration on shield, uniform, and horse. The main strength of the order's military might was its mounted knights, who acted as the foremost offensive arm. They wore scale armor, instead of plated armor, to improve mobility, speed, and striking power in the face of ever better-equipped, better-disciplined, and better-led infantry armies. Tannenberg was a cavalry battle, but one in which infantry and support forces played a vital role in the defeat of the hitherto invincible Teutonic Knights.

Teutons in open pitched battle in a confined space—as they were to do at Tannenberg—it was dubious whether they would be able to make a stand.

THE CAMPAIGN

In December 1409 during a meeting at Brest-Litovsk Jagiello, the Polish commanders and his cousin, Duke Witold, the Viceroy of Lithuania, agreed to combine their armies at a rendezvous on the Vistula, called Czerwinsk, where it was safe to cross the river barrier. It was safe from there to invade Prussia and hopefully defeat the Order on home ground. Meanwhile Jagiello secured the neutrality of the Order's Livonian knights while the friendly king of Hungary, who had signed an alliance with the Order, assured the Poles that he would not support his newfound allies. Thus the Commonwealth had no reason to fear a diversionary attack on their extensive southern and northeastern frontiers leaving them free to concentrate their considerable military strength against the Teutons.

To keep the Order's army (dispersed along the frontier) on its toes, Jagiello ordered diversionary offensives against Pomerania and Memel. In the meantime, using a 550-yard (600m) long pontoon bridge across the Vistula, the Poles and Lithuanians had combined at the Czerwinsk bridgehead by June 30. They marched northward on July 2. Ulrich von Jungingen, Grand Master of the Teutonic Order, had failed to concentrate his army because he underestimated his enemy in general and his technical expertise—he could not believe the "primitive" Poles and Lithuanians capable of building pontoon bridges! His racial arrogance was to cost him his life and the existence and reputation of his army as well. In a mere eight days the Royal Army had covered 82 miles (90km)—a phenomenal rate of advance for a medieval army—crossing the Prussian frontier already on July 2, 1410. Ulrich was caught by surprise again and was forced to concentrate his scattered army at Kurzetnik where, on July 3, Jagiello's army joined him. The two armies were now poised for battle.

DISPOSITIONS

Ulrich built a series of bridges across the Drweça River in order for his army to cross over to its eastern bank where the battlefield formed a rough triangle between three small Prussian villages—Tannenberg, Grünwald, and Ludwigsdorf. In this partly wooded and rough terrain visibility could have been better. The battlefield was shaped like a shallow soup dish measuring 1.9 miles (3km) in diameter.

Jagiello's combined army numbered 10,000–20,000 infantry and as many as 40,000 cavalry (including Tartar auxiliaries) while the Grand Master had 21,000 cavalry and a mere 6,000 infantry. The Royal Army's camp was situated 4.5 miles (7.2km) east of Grünwald at Lake Lubien while the Order's army had moved across the river into the field. At dawn on July 15 a Polish knight and scout, Hanko, entered the camp and informed Jagiello that the enemy was already drawn up for battle. Ulrich had caught the enemy—only forming up slowly—by surprise and should have, in hindsight, attacked immediately with all force and determination. Instead Ulrich ordered his men to dig ditches and form the army in two lines. His decision was the more faulty since here was open ground with good visibility well suited for a massed cavalry attack up to the slopes of the ridge that led to Lake Lubien and the Royal army's camp.

THE BATTLE

But nothing happened because Ulrich wanted the enemy to make the first move and they—primarily the cautious and shrewd Jagiello—were reluctant to act. As the morning hours wore on and his men grew impatient, Ulrich decided to goad the "cowardly" Poles and Lithuanians into action. He sent Duke Kazimir of Stettin (Szczeczin) whose shield bore the Black Eagle on a gold background (symbol of the Holy Roman Emperor) and the Imperial Herald to rebuke Jagiello for not fighting like a man. Jagiello, hoping to negotiate a peaceful settlement, received the two knights politely but was rudely told that his army should come out to fight like men on the

field of battle. Jagiello gave as good as he got, telling the two arrogant knights that they would regret their insults in a few hours and they, like the Grand Master, would get more than they had bargained for. He gave a signal for Witold to commence the battle.

The Poles advanced in good order on the left while the Lithuanians, Russians, and Tartars could not control themselves and threw themselves at the Germans who buckled under the onslaught. The Teutonic knights counter-attacked, slaying the enemy, and the Lithuanian army began to falter and retreat as the Tartars (either fleeing or executing a feigned retreat) moved out of range. Only Witold's central regiments held the line and Witold was forced, in person, to beg his cousin to save his flank.

Jagiello sent his last remaining reserves that managed to stem the Teutonic advance but as the dust settled Ulrich noticed how exposed the Polish king was on a small knoll on the battlefield, and sent a small force to either kill or capture Jagiello. The assassination attempt failed since some alert Polish knights saw what was happening and moved to intercept the Teutons. Witold used this time to rally his men who turned around and rode back to the center of the battlefield. It was the Teutons' turn to be caught unawares as Tartar arrows, Russian battleaxes, and Lithuanian swords cut

ABOVE: IN THIS ROMANTICIZED nineteenth-century oil painting by the Polish artist Maksymiljan Piotrowski (1813–75), the Polish-Lithuanians, led by their venerable-looking king, Wladislaw II, prepare for battle on July 15, 1410.

at them. The Poles, having held their line, forced the Order's knights back and surrounded them. Ulrich, stubborn, proud yet brave, chose like his men to stand and fight where they stood and as a consequence they were cut down. Few remained alive when the battle finally ended, at 7 P.M., at the village of Grünwald. Some 14,000 of the Order's knights and soldiers had been taken prisoner while the rest (18,000) lay strewn dead or dying on the dusty battlefield.

AFTERMATH

Instead of marching on the Teutonic Order's capital of Marienburg to the west, the utterly exhausted Polish-Lithuanian army remained on the battlefield to divide the loot, rest, and recuperate. When it was ready to march on Marienburg, held by Count Heinrich von Plauen and 3,000 troops, it was too late. This immense fortress complex with stone walls 27ft (8.2m) high and 7ft (2.1m) thick and ample supplies of food and water proved impregnable. Jagiello's victorious army arrived on July 25 but failed to make any headway during the two-month siege. The war would continue for years and the Order would eventually recover.

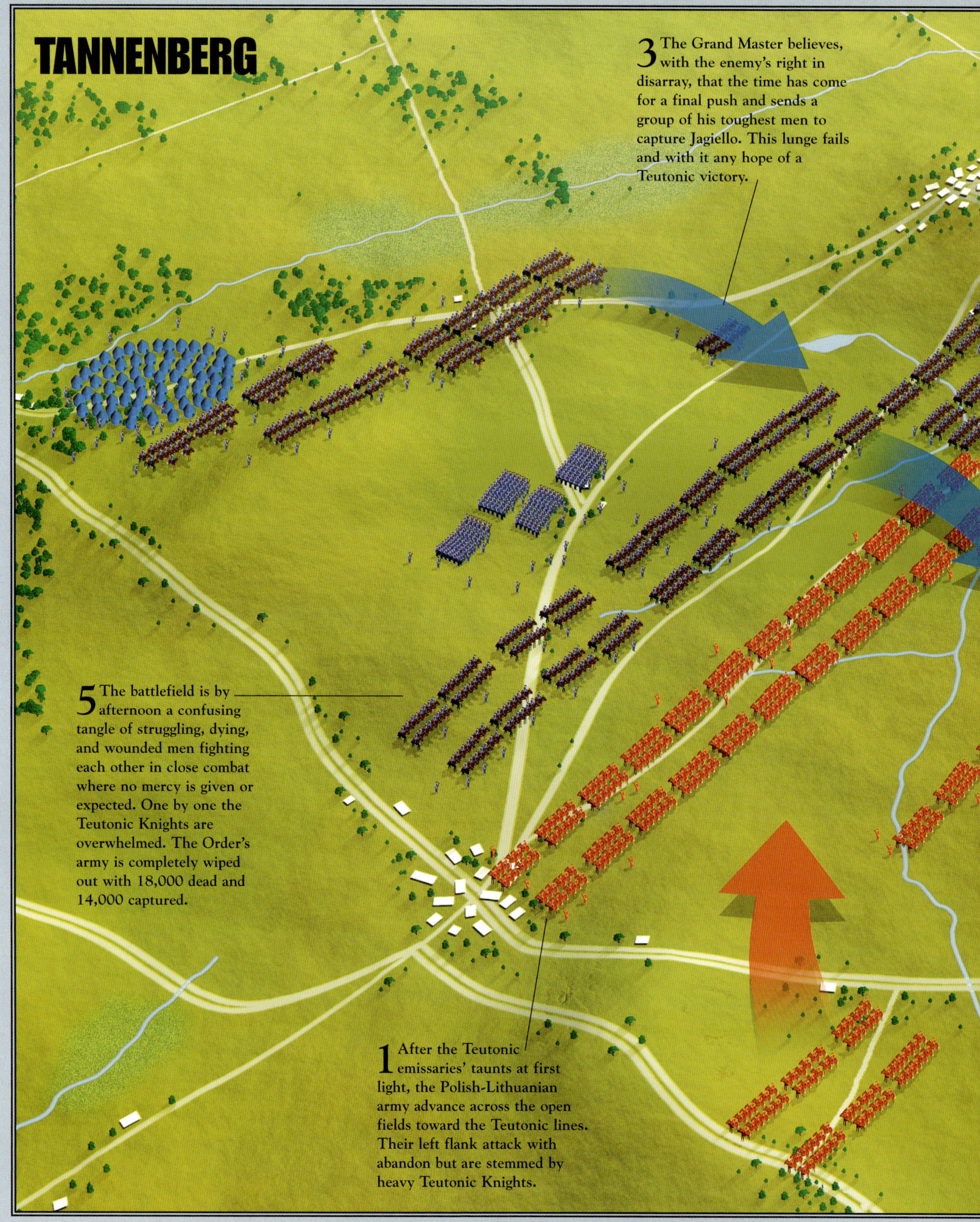
TANNENBERG

3 The Grand Master believes, with the enemy's right in disarray, that the time has come for a final push and sends a group of his toughest men to capture Jagiello. This lunge fails and with it any hope of a Teutonic victory.

5 The battlefield is by afternoon a confusing tangle of struggling, dying, and wounded men fighting each other in close combat where no mercy is given or expected. One by one the Teutonic Knights are overwhelmed. The Order's army is completely wiped out with 18,000 dead and 14,000 captured.

1 After the Teutonic emissaries' taunts at first light, the Polish-Lithuanian army advance across the open fields toward the Teutonic lines. Their left flank attack with abandon but are stemmed by heavy Teutonic Knights.

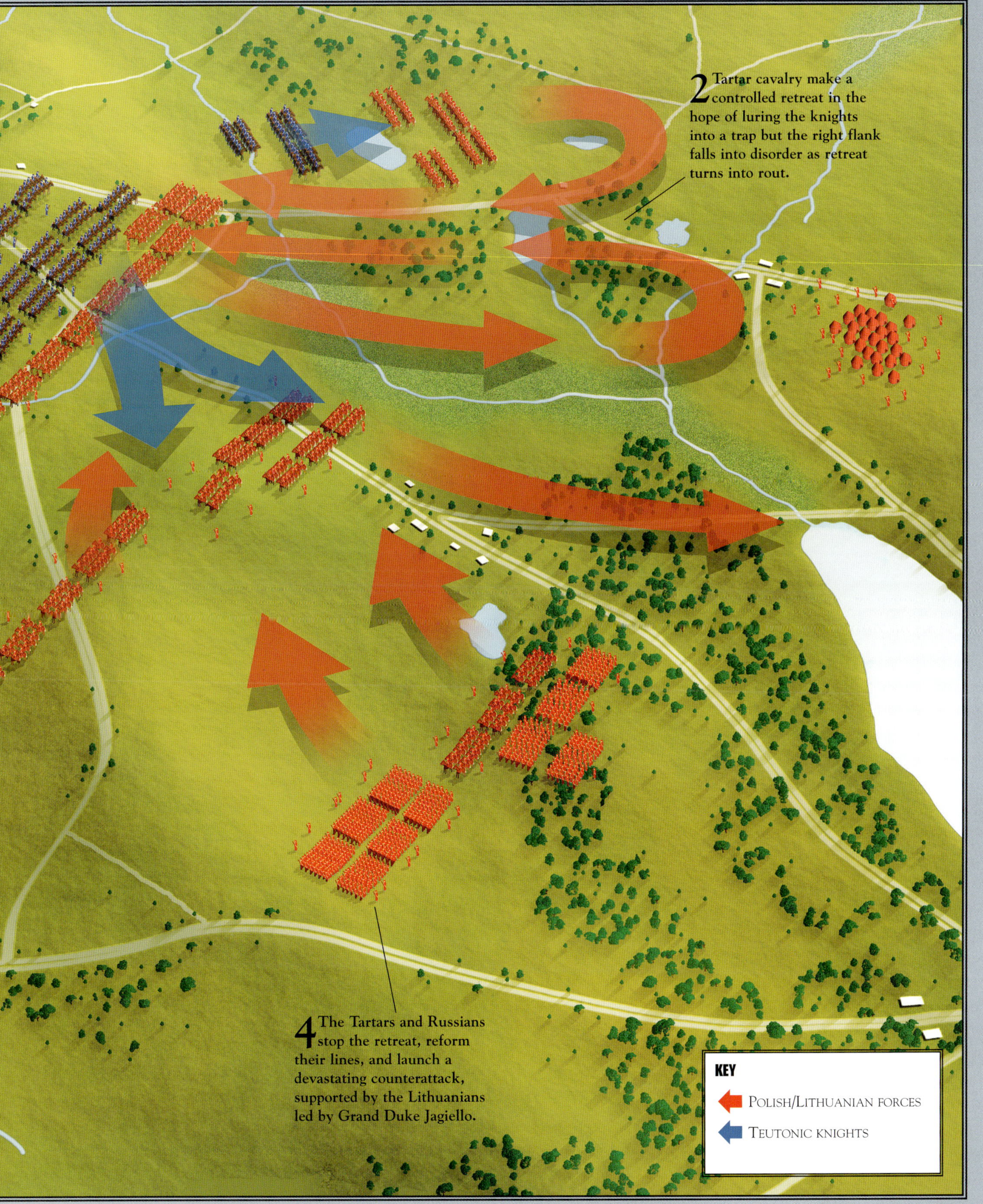
2 Tartar cavalry make a controlled retreat in the hope of luring the knights into a trap but the right flank falls into disorder as retreat turns into rout.
4 The Tartars and Russians stop the retreat, reform their lines, and launch a devastating counterattack, supported by the Lithuanians led by Grand Duke Jagiello.
KEY
Polish/Lithuanian forces
Teutonic knights

THE GREAT ARMADA

1588

The defeat of the Spanish Armada is one of the legendary victories of English history. English gunnery overcame a Spanish fleet equipped for boarding actions, but only after an attack by fireships at Calais scattered the Armada, preventing it from escorting the Spanish army across the Channel.

Until 1585 King Philip II of Spain and Queen Elizabeth I had learned to live with each other. In that year, Francis Drake raided the Spanish coast while the English, now allied to the Dutch rebels, landed 4,000 troops in Holland. It was a declaration of war, if not in name, then in reality against Spain. Parma suggested that he should land 30,000 men from his Army of Flanders directly on the Kent coast while Don Álvaro de Bazán, Marquis of Santa Cruz, suggested sending 510 ships and 95,000 troops against England directly from Spain. Santa Cruz had taken

ARMADA FACTS

Who: Philip II of Spain sent the Duke of Medina Sidonia (1550–1619) with the "invincible Armada" against Queen Elizabeth I of England whose fleet was led by Lord Howard of Effingham (1536–1624) and Sir Francis Drake (1543–96).

What: A landmark naval battle that saw the English system of sea warfare with battle lines firing broadsides introduced, eclipsing the tactics of Spanish "galley style" warfare.

Where: The English Channel from Cornwall to Gravelines on the Belgian coast.

When: July 31 to August 9, 1588.

Why: Philip II was seeking to invade England with the Duke of Parma's 30,000-strong army and end his English problems once and for all.

Outcome: A fireship attack at Calais broke up the Armada's formation, the English won the engagement at Gravelines, and the survivors of the Armada were forced to sail around the British Isles to escape.

LEFT: THIS COLORFUL HAND-TINTED ILLUSTRATION *shows the Spanish and English fleet closing with each other in the English Channel in August 1588. From a painting in the National Maritime Museum.*

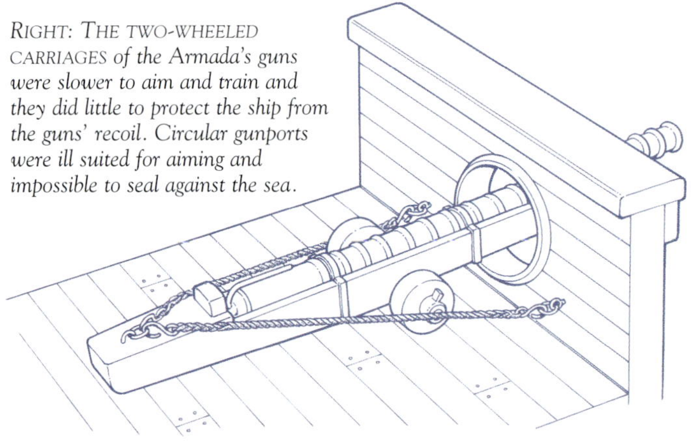

RIGHT: THE TWO-WHEELED CARRIAGES of the Armada's guns were slower to aim and train and they did little to protect the ship from the guns' recoil. Circular gunports were ill suited for aiming and impossible to seal against the sea.

the Portuguese islands of the Azores (1582–3) and had fought at Lepanto in 1571 when the Holy League crushed the Turkish fleet. Hesitant and cautious by nature, Philip II chose a compromise between the two. He would send the Armada into the Channel to then escort Parma across from the Netherlands. This strategic compromise would prove the undoing of the Armada before it even left port.

To gain time for English anti-invasion preparations the famous English buccaneer (or pirate as the Spanish referred to him) Sir Francis Drake set sail with 22 ships and on April 19, 1587 attacked Cadiz where he burnt or captured 36 Spanish vessels at anchor, and in May raided the Azores. Drake's dangerous presence forced Philip to delay the sailing of the Armada until the following spring.

LEFT: THIS PORTRAIT (c. 1620) shows Lord Howard of Effingham, Earl of Nottingham (1536–1624), the Lord High Admiral who led the English fleet against the Spanish Armada.

Philip II had appointed Santa Cruz to command the Armada but the Marquis died in February 1588 in the middle of the preparations. Santa Cruz's place as Captain-General of the Ocean Sea was taken by the 38-year-old Don Alonso Pérez de Guzman, the seventh Duke of Medina Sidonia—an experienced and efficient organizer who soon had the massive Armada project back on track. Whatever the Duke lacked in terms of actual combat experience he made up for in cool tactical and strategic skills, common sense, stern discipline, and ruthless determination. He set about with tremendous energy to repair the damage wrought by Drake's raids and the chaos that Santa Cruz had left behind.

THE ARMADA SAILS

On April 1 the Duke received Philip II's orders: he was to sail to Margate in support of Parma, who was to land at Ramsgate and march along the Thames to take London. Once this had been achieved Philip would force Elizabeth I to make concessions. Philip very perceptively warned Medina Sidonia that the English would seek to avoid close combat and would use their superiority in naval gunnery to sink or damage the Duke's ships.

On May 30, 1588 the Armada, numbering 130 ships with 2,400 guns, 8,000 sailors, and 19,000 troops, set sail from Lisbon. The Armada may have looked formidable at a distance, but it was far weaker than it appeared. The Spanish treated war at sea like an extension of land warfare. Their experience of sea warfare was gained fighting the Turks in the Mediterranean. However, that was with galley fleets where ships were boarded by heavily armed troops, which was why the Spanish carried so many troops aboard their ships. The Spanish hoped to close with the English ships, sink their grappling hooks into them and then carry the enemy ships by boarding.

THE ENGLISH FLEET

The English, however, sought to fight in a completely different way. They had learnt to build fast, sleek galleons with plenty of medium and heavy guns and the English would rely upon firepower and speed to outrun, outgun, and outmaneuver the slower and clumsier Spanish ships. The English had several other advantages compared to their enemy. They were fighting in defense of their country against a ruthless would-be invader who wished to impose his rule and religion upon them. This spurred them on. They were also fighting in home waters, the Channel, which they knew well. The Spanish were not familiar with these cold, gray waters and as attackers were not as motivated.

The English had also something resembling professional and specialized crews and officers. The captains were supreme commanders on their ships while on the Spanish ships command was divided between the military and naval officers where it was often unclear who had precedence. This caused not only confusion but fanned the flames of discord between the officers and troops/crew. The English had a well trained corps of gunners on board used to loading, firing, and reloading their guns swiftly and efficiently despite the rolling decks, while the Spanish used their army artillerists to do this. The English rate of fire was, therefore, three to four times faster than that of their enemy's.

Finally the ships themselves were quite different. Not even Philip II could afford a standing fleet on the scale of the Armada so most of the vessels had been hired or lent by individuals or friendly powers. Most of the Spanish tonnage was neither suited nor fitted out for a proper sea battle and the largest vessels (in the supply fleet) were not properly armed. By contrast the English vessels were specifically designed as warships, built for fighting in home waters, and for fast and intense fighting at short range. In 1588 the English had 24 newly constructed or fitted-out vessels in the Royal Navy and to this number could be added privateers and merchant ships. In total the English navy, under Charles Lord Howard of Effingham, numbered 105 vessels and the main fleet under Howard was anchored at Plymouth. Aged 52, Howard had in fact little experience of sea warfare or high command but his subordinates, such as Drake and Frobisher, had plenty from their numerous privateering raids against the enemy. Drake had divined, from whatever source, that the Armada would sail up the Channel and try to neutralize its English foe before Parma landed in England.

So far so good, from an English point of view, but they had no idea where Parma would land. Elizabeth had convinced herself they would land in Essex placing her favorite Robert Dudley, Earl of Leicester, with the bulk of the English army (14,000–20,000 men) there. That left only 4,000 poorly equipped levies to guard the Kent coast where in fact Parma's veterans were going to land.

THE FIRST DAY

Having been delayed at Corunna by a storm that temporarily scattered the huge fleet on July 19–21, the Armada sailed slowly across the Bay of Biscay and on July 30 entered the

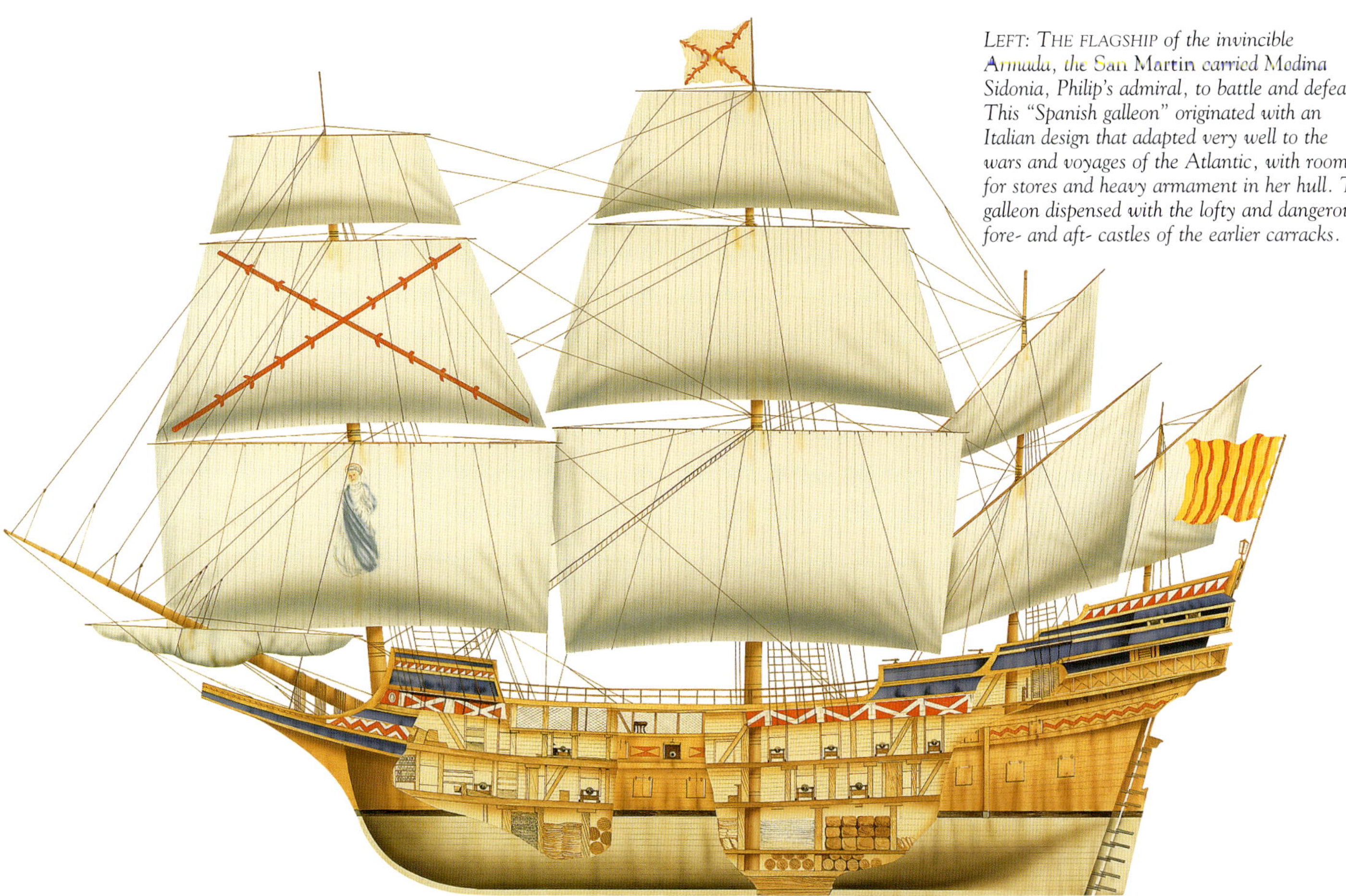

LEFT: THE FLAGSHIP of the invincible Armada, the San Martin carried Medina Sidonia, Philip's admiral, to battle and defeat. This "Spanish galleon" originated with an Italian design that adapted very well to the wars and voyages of the Atlantic, with room for stores and heavy armament in her hull. The galleon dispensed with the lofty and dangerous fore- and aft- castles of the earlier carracks.

RIGHT: APART FROM HIS *military exploits, Sir Francis Drake was well known as a successful pirate who preyed upon Spanish shipping. In his role as an explorer, he was also the first English sailor to circumnavigate the globe, from 1577–80.*

Channel. During the night of July 30/31 Howard's fleet of 64 ships sailed across the path of the advancing Armada while Drake's squadron was left inshore. Medina Sidonia formed his vast Armada into a huge crescent where he commanded the center (90 ships). The left flank (20 ships) was under the command of Don Alonso Martinez de Leiva and the right flank (also 20 ships) under Don Juan Martinez de Recalde. The whole battle formation spread out some 2 miles (3.2km) from the tip of the left horn to the tip of the right. It was an impressive and terrifying sight.

As no formal declaration of war had been made between England and Spain, Howard sent out the appropriately named *Defiance* to fire a token shot at the approaching Armada. This was the signal for battle to commence. As Howard's fleet prepared for battle it was the turn of the Spanish to be perturbed as the English ships turned in a formation *en ala*, a line. This was the new flexible system of giving battle at sea attacking the enemy using a broadside. The English were sensible and cautious avoiding all close contact with the Spanish ships. They had good reason to be careful as the Spanish ships were packed with men armed with grappling hooks, ropes, and hand grenades at the ready. In close hand-to-hand combat the lightly armed English sailors and crews stood little chance.

FURTHER ENGAGEMENTS

The following day (August 1) Don Pedro de Valdés in the crippled *Nuestra Senora del Rosario*—having been abandoned by the rest of the Armada—was forced to strike at Drake aboard the *Revenge*. Drake's many English detractors believed he had veered off during the night in order to seize the *Nuestra Senora* as a prize.

During the previous day's fighting some of the Spanish captains had wavered in holding their positions in the rigid battle formation and in the light of this Medina Sidonia gave orders that any commander who broke ranks would be hanged without mercy for cowardice. Then he divided the command: he would lead the vanguard in person while Leiva brought up the rear, and to steady the nerves of his crews and officers he created two heavy battle groups with the largest and gunned vessels in his Fleet.

On August 2, as the Armada was west of Portland Bill, Howard attacked again and the English found however that their fire had little effect. They fired 500 rounds at the *San Martin* without causing any serious damage. Howard broke off

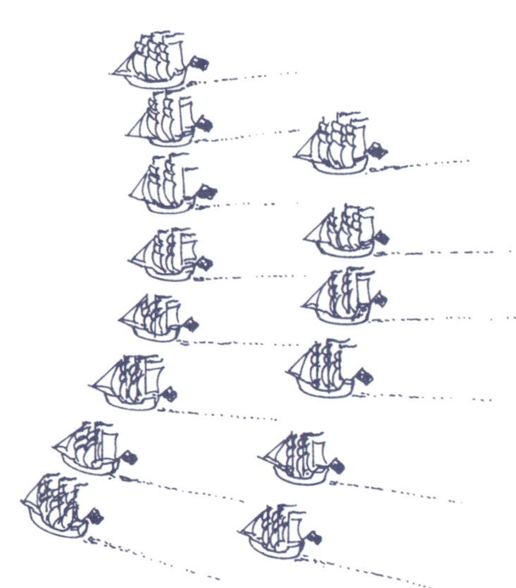

ABOVE: LINE OF SIGHT *limited the formations of the era into two basic shapes: line of battle (ships side to side with their bows to the enemy) or column (ships proceeding bow to stern toward the foe). The ships in line of battle have the options, wind or sea permitting, to present their broadsides to the advancing foe. The ships in column can close the range and attempt to sail through the enemy's formation or they may turn suddenly to form a line of battle of their own.*

the battle because his ships were running out of ammunition, noting that the Armada seemed, after all, invincible. By the evening Medina Sidonia contemplated sailing into the Solent to capture Portsmouth and use it as a base. Howard was determined to prevent this and divided his fleet into four squadrons, each commanded by himself, Drake, Hawkins, and Frobisher. While the other three squadrons detained the Armada, Drake went out into the Channel, turned and attacked unexpectedly. The English forced the Armada to abandon its attack on the Solent and it drifted into the Channel again. A Spanish victory turned into a crucial English success. Nevertheless, the Armada was left unmolested for two days and reached Calais by the afternoon on August 6.

FIRESHIPS

Calais was a dubious sanctuary for the hard-pressed Spanish since the harbor was shallow and open with hardly any natural defenses against an English attack. However, in the ongoing religious civil war in France between Catholics and Protestants, the port of Calais was in the hands of the former, and the French governor was an ardent Catholic who welcomed the Armada with open arms. That same evening Parma's courier arrived by pinnace from his headquarters with the grim news that he would not be ready for another six days. Medina Sidonia realized the English and their Dutch allies—with 140 vessels hovering off the coast—would be most unlikely to give them that long.

His hunch was right as Howard had called a Council of War aboard his flagship the *Ark Royal* during the morning of August 7 where it was decided to send some eight fireships against the anchored Armada. Howard hoped to spread confusion and disorder thus enabling the English to move to point-blank range and blast the Spanish vessels. His scheme went according to plan. Medina Sidonia had suspected the English would launch an attack with fireships and posted lookouts so when the attack was launched during the night of August 7/8 two of the English craft were intercepted and ran aground. That left six that got through. The English had loaded the vessels' gun barrels with double shot, so the explosion, the smoke, and fire were tremendous, spreading panic and fear. Most captains of the Armada cut their cables in a wild and thoughtless scramble to get away and save their skins despite the Duke's orders to save the anchors and return to their previous positions once the attack was over.

By dawn on August 8 the Duke was left with his flagship and only four escorts to protect him. Little by little the vessels returned with the heavily armed galleons protecting the scattered Armada's rear as the Spanish vessels reformed. The stark truth, however, was that the English had them where they wanted them—strung out along the shallow coastal waters of Flanders. At last the English could use their superior firepower at point-blank range with devastating effect. The battle of Gravelines (August 8) was fought in the shoal waters between Gravelines and Ostend, lasting nine hours. The *San Martin* received 200 shot, was badly damaged and began to take on water while her Portuguese sister-ship, the *San Mateo*, was riddled with English shot. Both vessels ran aground between Nieuwpoort and Ostend where they and their crews were captured by the Dutch. Two more vessels, including the *El Gran Grifon* ran aground while one, the *Maria Juan*, was actually sunk—the only one to be so.

AFTERMATH

The Spanish had 1,000 dead and 800 wounded and morale collapsed. Medina Sidonia made desperate efforts to gather his ships by signaling and then he called his remaining captains together. They failed to convince the Duke as to why they had not returned to the Armada and he simply turned to the Provost with an icy order: "Hang the traitors." As it was they were all spared except one, Don Cristobal de Avila, who was hanged from the yard arm and then his corpse was put into a pinnace on display to restore order and discipline.

The Armada had lost the battle against the English and now, with discipline restored, made the arduous and amazing trip around the British Isles back to Spain. It was a measure of Medina Sidonia's leadership and his men's fortitude and toughness that so many ships made it back at all.

NAVAL GUN CARRIAGE

The wheels of this gun carriage allowed the cannon's recoil to expend itself in movement, rather than in damaging a vessel's timbers, while gunners could elevate the weapon by movement of the wooden wedge beneath the breech. Reloading tackles also allowed the cannon to be trained from the side. Carriages of this design enabled the British to achieve a superior rate of fire during the Armada battles.

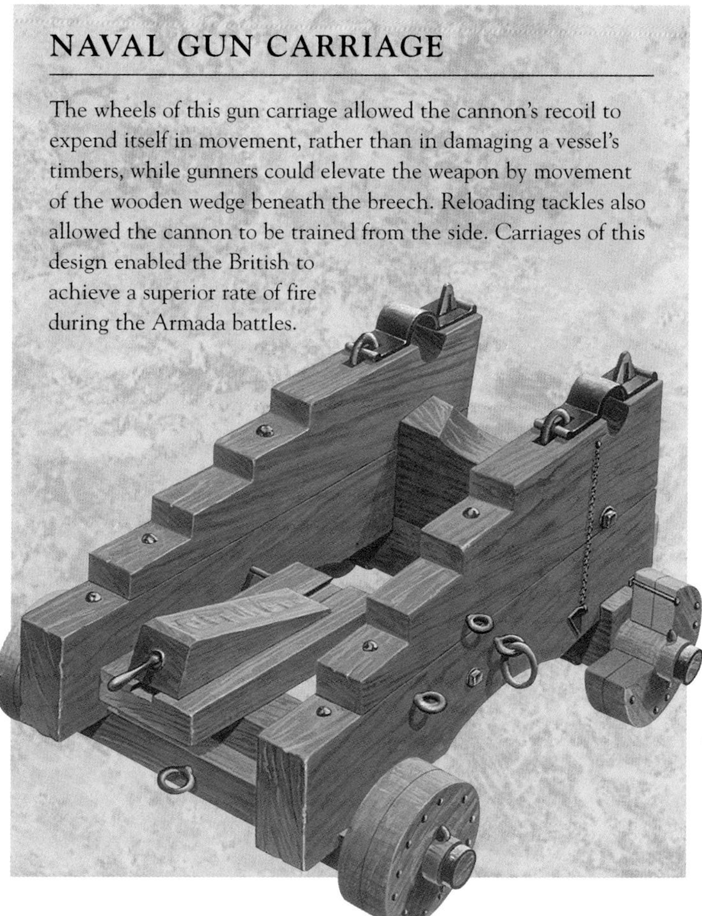

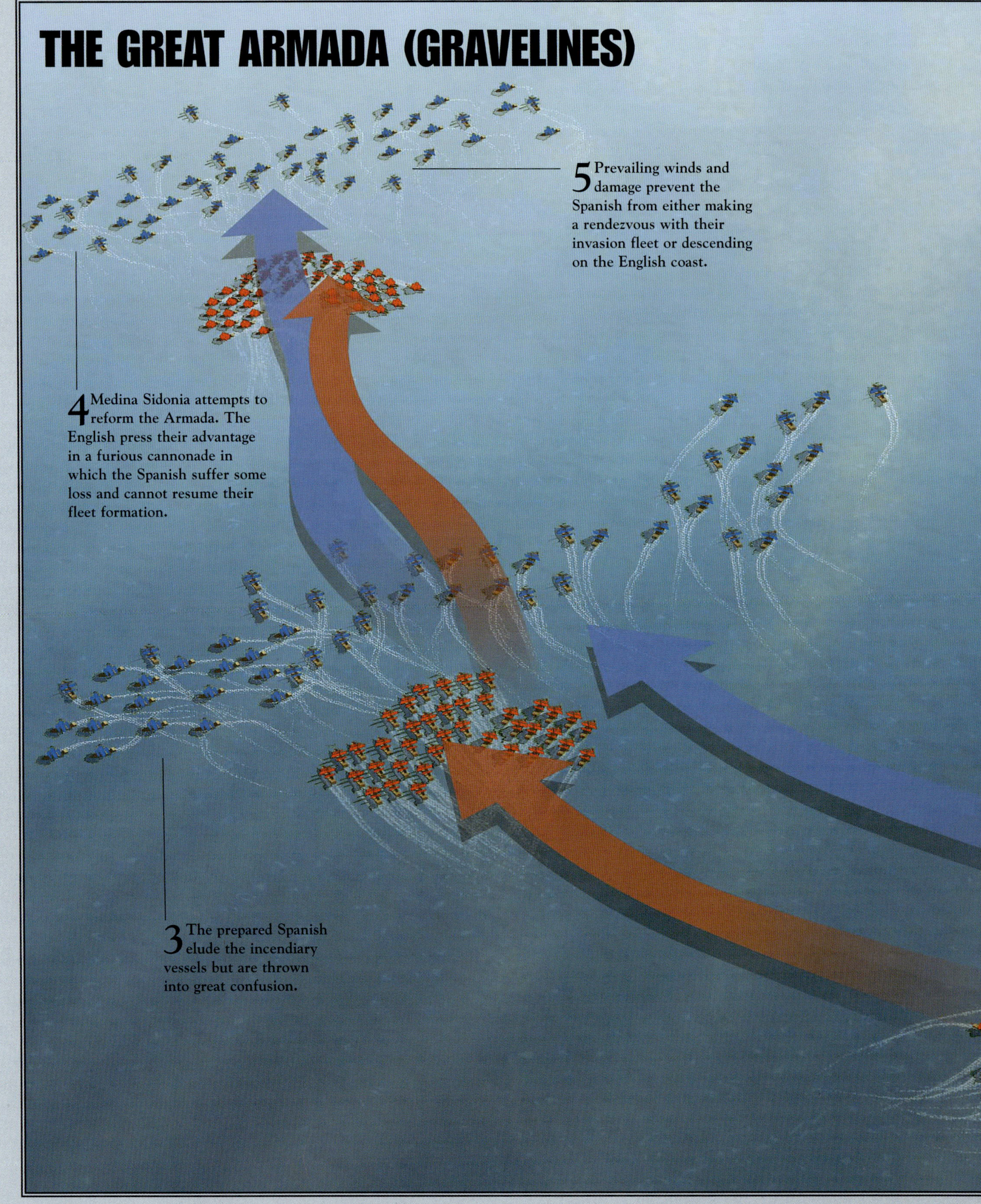
THE GREAT ARMADA (GRAVELINES)
5 Prevailing winds and damage prevent the Spanish from either making a rendezvous with their invasion fleet or descending on the English coast.
4 Medina Sidonia attempts to reform the Armada. The English press their advantage in a furious cannonade in which the Spanish suffer some loss and cannot resume their fleet formation.
3 The prepared Spanish elude the incendiary vessels but are thrown into great confusion.

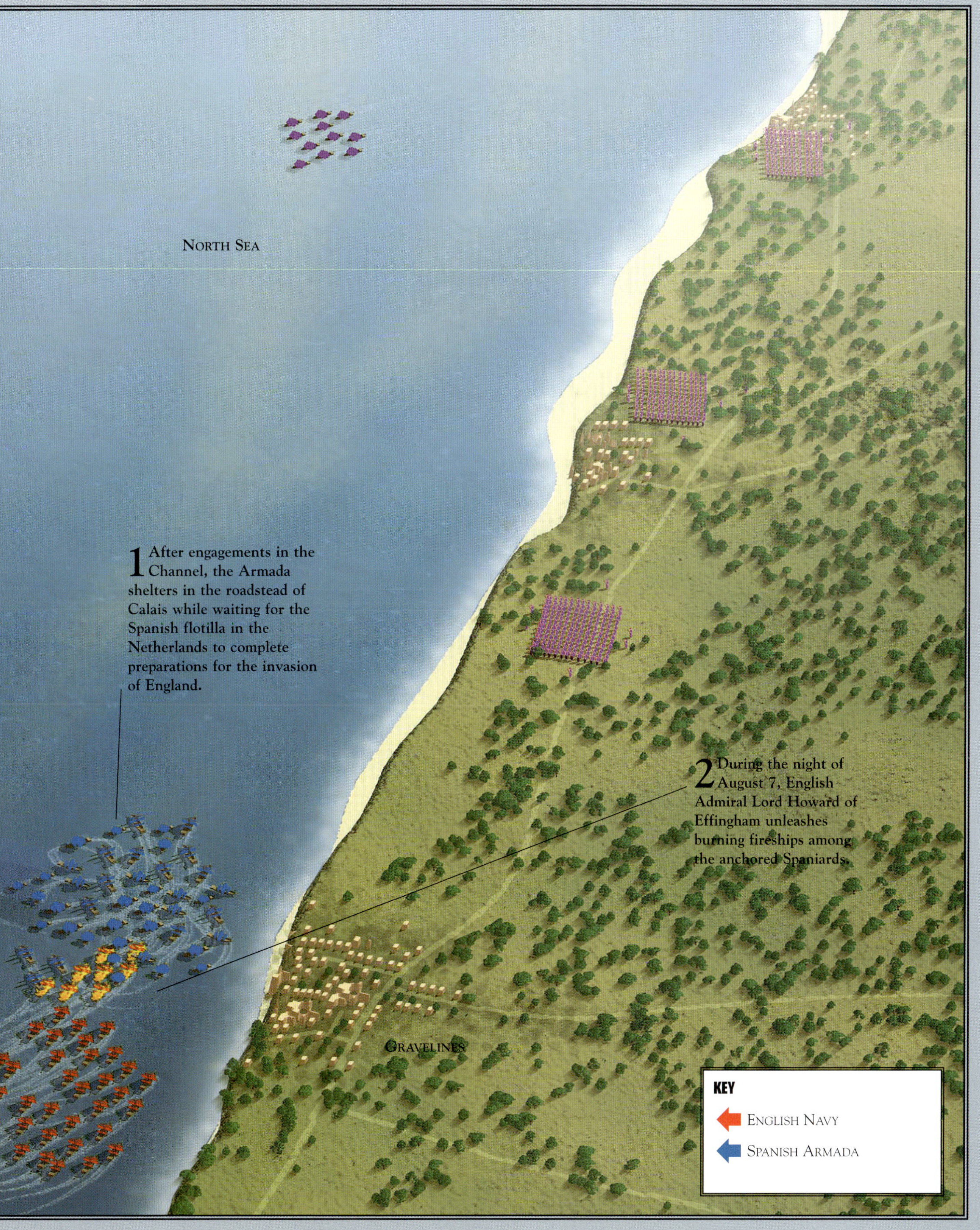
NORTH SEA
1 After engagements in the Channel, the Armada shelters in the roadstead of Calais while waiting for the Spanish flotilla in the Netherlands to complete preparations for the invasion of England.
2 During the night of August 7, English Admiral Lord Howard of Effingham unleashes burning fireships among the anchored Spaniards.
GRAVELINES
KEY
ENGLISH NAVY
SPANISH ARMADA

TRAFALGAR 1805

Nelson's victory at Trafalgar finally ended the threat of French invasion of the British Isles and secured the Royal Navy's dominance of the seas for the next 100 years. But at the moment of his greatest triumph, Britain's foremost naval hero was killed on the deck of his flagship HMS Victory.

Nelson's victory at Trafalgar 200 years ago is the most famous and decisive naval battle of all times. But, often forgotten, is that it was the product of Napoleon's plans to invade Britain. By the spring of 1805 Napoleon had assembled some 2,000 gunboats and transports in the French Channel ports to ferry an army of 167,000 veteran troops to the coast of Kent. For the invasion to succeed Napoleon had to be sure the Royal Navy was safely lured out of the Channel when his ramshackle flotilla of barges and flat-bottomed boats sailed out of Boulogne and Calais.

Napoleon had a justified contempt for his own navy but this time he needed its support if he was to destroy his most dangerous foe. Unfortunately, Napoleon had a knack for appointing the wrong men to crucial posts when it came to sea warfare and

TRAFALGAR FACTS

Who: The combined Franco-Spanish fleet of 33 ships of the line under Admiral Pierre Villeneuve (1763–1806) versus a British fleet of 27 ships of the line under Vice Admiral Lord Horatio Nelson (1758–1805).

What: Nelson's head-on attack on the Franco-Spanish line broke their formation and allowed the superior gunnery of the British ships to destroy the enemy in detail.

Where: At the western entrance to the Straits of Gibraltar off Cape Trafalgar, Spain.

When: October 21, 1805.

Why: Nelson, having chased the Franco-Spanish Fleet around the world, caught up with it in the Straits of Gibraltar and Villeneuve chose—for personal reasons—to fight rather than flee.

Outcome: The Combined Fleet, despite heroic resistance, was smashed and Britain had removed, for good, the threat of a French invasion.

Left: This print, after the painting, "Trafalgar" by William Overend, was published in the Illustrated Sporting and Dramatic News *in 1905 with the title, "'The Hero of Trafalgar' Nelson on Board the Victory, October 21st 1805." Nelson is shown standing on the right on the deck of the* Victory, *facing fixedly ahead while the battle rages around him.*

RIGHT: LORD HORATIO NELSON, as painted by Sir William Beechey (1753–1839), the English landscape and portrait painter.

when he picked Count Pierre Villeneuve he had truly excelled himself. Not only had he survived Aboukir Bay (1798), thus acquiring a life-long terror of Nelson, but Villeneuve detested Napoleon's person and politics. Villeneuve, quite rightly, did not think much of Napoleon's confused and wooly ideas when it came to naval strategy—and especially his plan to lure Nelson to the West Indies with Villeneuve's squadron that sailed out of Toulon on March 30. At that very time Nelson was sailing in the balmy Mediterranean waters between Sardinia and Sicily expecting Villeneuve to set sail for Egypt. It was only on April 18 that he knew that the French fleet was heading west into the Atlantic.

On May 12, with 10 ships of the line and three frigates Nelson headed out into the Atlantic bound for the West Indies. Four days later Villeneuve had reached Martinique where he was determined to stay until Admiral Ganteaume with his 21 sail of the line joined him from Brest. But Villeneuve had to begin sailing back to European waters to support Napoleon's landings by June 22 at the latest. On May 26 six Spanish ships of the line under the command of Admiral Federico Gravina (1757–1806) joined them, bringing the Combined Fleet to 21 ships of the line.

CALDER'S ACTION

Meanwhile Nelson had again been fed faulty intelligence, so when he reached the West Indies he sailed south to Trinidad rather than north. He had missed the elusive enemy again. Nelson's colleague, the Channel Fleet commander, Admiral Sir Robert Calder (1745–1845), had more luck because he ran into the Combined Fleet at Cape Finisterre on July 22. Calder had 15 ships of the line facing Villeneuve's 21 ships of the line and seven frigates. An indecisive action, hampered by thick fog, ensued in which Calder captured two Spanish ships and damaged four others, while suffering only four ships damaged and 199 casualties among his own squadron. Both fleets sailed off in opposite directions on July 27.

Although Calder thought he had done well, the failure to destroy the Combined Fleet led to criticism at home, and Calder demanded a court-martial to clear his name. Calder's only consolation was that Villeneuve's performance was considered even worse.

Ungraciously the French commander blamed Gravina and the Spanish for the defeat at Finisterre when in fact the Spanish had fought splendidly, as Napoleon—an inveterate Hispanophobe—had to admit a month later.

LEFT: DEATH FROM ABOVE could come from weapons such as this coehoorn mortar in platforms called "fighting tops." Fire from marine marksmen and blasts of shot could clear the upper decks of an enemy warship, rendering her immobile, or "decapitate" a foe by selective fire at officers.

NELSON AT CADIZ

Nelson had nothing to celebrate either as he returned one last time to England on August 19. He had expected boos and catcalls but he was feted and praised on all sides. Even the stone-faced Premier, William Pitt, gave him his full backing. The same day that Nelson returned to take command of the British blockading squadron at Cadiz—September 29—the Admiral celebrated his 47th birthday. He looked, with his almost white hair, sunken face, and small, maimed body at least a decade older.

Old-looking he may have been but Nelson was his usual fighting self. He perked up when Pitt's promise of aid was quite unexpectedly fulfilled—by October 15 Nelson had some 27 ships of the line and five frigates. The frigates were under the command of Captain Sir Henry Blackwood (1770–1832), standing off some 3 miles (4.8km) from shore to keep an eye on the Combined Fleet in Cadiz. The Combined Fleet numbered 2,600 sailors and 33 ships of the line to Nelson's 27 ships and 2,100 sailors. (Most of Nelson's ships, despite the supposed ubiquity of the press gangs, were undermanned compared to the enemy.)

Nelson planned that, once the Combined Fleet sailed out of Cadiz, he would attack the enemy in two columns at right angles to their line, thus breaking it up and then isolating and destroying the rearmost part before the vanguard could support it. Nelson may have thought this was a "secret" plan but Villeneuve—who had studied Nelson closely—realized immediately that this was what Nelson was going to do. Villeneuve may have been a timid and uninspiring commander of men, but he was no fool, and his actions on October 21 proved he was no coward either.

DISPOSITIONS

The Combined Fleet began to sail out of Cadiz during the early hours of Saturday October 19 but they had only reached the entrance of the Straits of Gibraltar two days later. The Franco-Spanish battle line, if one could call it that, was a straggling and scattered confusion of ships 9 miles (14.4km) long. This morning, Monday October 21, would be fateful for both sides as a growing groundswell gave indication of an Atlantic storm coming their way.

Originally heading into the Mediterranean, Villeneuve gave orders for the entire fleet to reverse course because he was determined to die in battle and not have to face the odious Corsican's wrath should he escape to Naples. By 10 A.M. his fleet—in the shape of an irregular crescent with wide spaces between the vessels—had finally changed direction. Admiral Le Pelley's Division now formed the vanguard while Gravina's tough Spaniards—who should have been in the lead—became the rearguard. An hour later Villeneuve observed how Nelson's fleet bore down on them in two separate columns readying themselves for battle.

GUN DECK

Three-tiered gundecks marked the "First Rate" capital ships of the Age of Fighting Sail. On the top deck the loaded cannon is run out on its truck through the open gun port, ready to fire upon the approaching enemy. The middle deck depicts a fired cannon rolling back into the ship from the recoil of its shot, where it will be cleaned and reloaded by the gun crew. The lowest deck shows a gun secured against the closed gun port for sea worthiness. A "loose cannon" was more than metaphorically dangerous in a ship rolling and pitching in heavy weather.

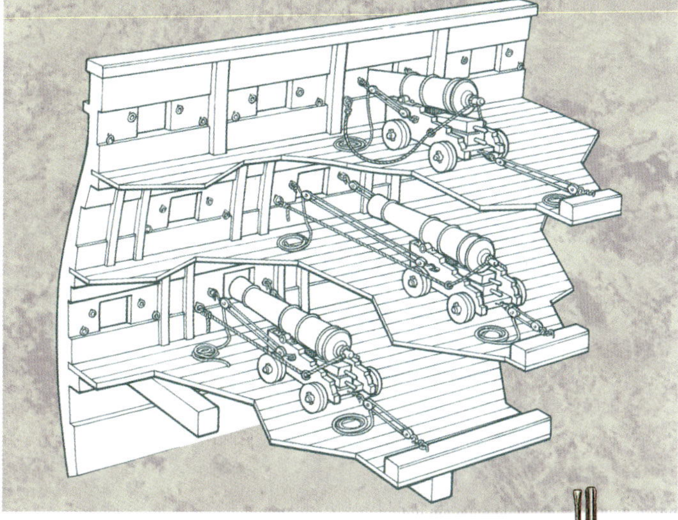

As for the British they had readied themselves for battle since 6 A.M. Nelson was determined to give chase and catch up with the fleeing Combined Fleet in order to destroy Napoleon's naval arm. To his and the other British commanders' utter astonishment the enemy, at 8:40 A.M. reversed direction, and headed back west—straight at them! As usual, Nelson was determined to take the lead with HMS *Victory* (his 100-gun flagship) but his commanders warned him that this would make him a sitting target for the enemy's fire. Nelson brushed aside the idea that he should let

RIGHT: ALL NAVIES of the period used onboard marines to pour musket fire on the crews of enemy ships from the rigging. It is a French marine from the Redoutable *that is thought to have killed Nelson when the two ships were engaged in a point-blank exchange of fire.*

ABOVE: THREE TIERS OF GUNS *protrude from the side of HMS* Victory. *First laid down in 1759, HMS* Victory *was a first-rate ship of the line with 100 guns and a complement of more than 850 men. In July 1803, she became Admiral Nelson's flagship, and he is said to have only spent 25 days off the ship from that time until his death.*

his deputy Admiral Collingwood's squadron take the lead. The winds were west-north-west, favoring the British and the clouds were gray and compact as the distance between the enemy fleets shrank with alarming rapidity. At 11 A.M. Nelson hoisted a unique but morale-boosting, if patently obvious, signal to his Fleet: "England expects that every man will do his duty." There was an almighty roar of approval from officers and men across the British fleet as the signal was read and understood.

THE BATTLE

Forty-five minutes later the first hesitant firing began as Villeneuve, on his flagship *Bucentaure* (80 guns), gingerly hoisted his pennant. Nelson, by contrast, was on the poop deck of the *Victory*, as he made—at 11:50 A.M.—his last signal for the Fleet to "Engage the enemy more closely." By 12:04 P.M. *Victory*'s massive oak sides were being showered with shot from *Bucentaure* (concentrating her fire against Victory's port quarter), *Redoutable*, *Héros*, and the Spanish behemoth—the 136-gun *Santissíma Trinidad*, the flagship of Admiral Baltazar de Cisneros.

While these fired broadsides against *Victory* the French and Spanish sharpshooters on the decks and in the masts swept *Victory*'s decks with musket fire. *Victory*'s wheel was smashed, forcing her to be steered from below deck, Nelson's secretary John Scott was killed, the mizzen topmast was shot away, and all the other masts were damaged. *Victory* finally passed under the stern of the *Bucentaure*, and unleashed a devastating double-shotted raking broadside through her stern galleries, dismounting 20 guns and killing dozens of her crew. The rest of the fleet followed, breaking the Franco-Spanish line just as Nelson had planned and the battle became a mêlée of individual ship-to-ship actions where superior British gunnery would dominate.

By 1:10 P.M. *Victory* was entangled with the French *Redoutable* commanded by Captain Jean-Jacques Lucas—a firebrand Provençal—who inspired his crew to fight ferociously against their British enemy. In a matter of minutes the accurate and deadly French fire had killed 40 marines. A sharpshooter aboard the *Redoutable* hit Nelson with a shot that penetrated the Admiral's shoulder, lung, and pierced his spine.

Now and for the next two hours the battle was at its fiercest. The *Redoubtable* was now under fire from both sides as the 98-gun HMS *Téméraire* joined the fight. At 1:40 P.M. the *Téméraire* raked the *Redoubtable*—by now a wreck—with repeated broadsides but Lucas and his brave crew refused to

LEFT: CANNON OF CAST IRON *mounted on rolling wooden trucks were a cheap and functional weapon for every size of warship. Broad wheels let the cannon roll over the gundecks while crews checked the recoil with hawsers. The corkscrew-like worm, shown left, was used to remove the burning remnants of the expended powder bag, and the sponge and bucket used to wash the gun out.*

ABOVE: "THE DEATH OF NELSON" by Daniel Maclise (1806–70). This large painting shows Nelson after he was shot by a sniper on board the French ship Redoubtable. *He must have been a visible target in his dress uniform of Vice Admiral, despite the smoke of battle.*

strike their colors until *Téméraire* was in as equally miserable a shape as their own vessel. Finally Lucas and his men—utterly exhausted—surrendered. The *Redoutable* ship had lost 487 killed and 81 wounded including Lucas—a staggering 88 percent of its crew!

By 2:30 P.M. the *Santissíma Trinidad* too was a complete wreck but when a British boarding party stepped onto the deck a Spanish officer told them that the proud flagship had not capitulated despite being unable to fire a single gun. It would be hours until she was finally seized by the British. *Bucentaure* was also, by 4:15 P.M., out of commission with 450 casualties, hardly a crew member still standing, her three captains wounded.

Villeneuve, who had been standing completely still during the whole ordeal hoping with all his heart to be killed, did not have a scratch on him when his crippled flagship surrendered to Captain Israel Pellew of the *Conqueror*. Fifteen minutes later, at 4:30 P.M., his surgeon William Beatty being unable to do anything for him, Nelson died knowing that his beloved fleet had won a great victory. By this time Collingwood had smashed most of the Spanish squadron under Admiral Gravina, well to the southwest of the main battle area. The Spanish, like the French, put up a ferocious defense of their ships but were in the end defeated by the more experienced British.

AFTERMATH

At the end of the battle, 17 ships of the Combined Fleet were in British hands, and another one was a blazing wreck. Of the 15 survivors, four were taken at the battle of Cape Ortegal on November 4 and only 11 made it back to Cadiz under the badly wounded Gravina. A storm blew up after the battle, however, forcing the British to scuttle many of their hard-won prizes.

The news of Nelson's victory reached England on November 6, where rejoicing at the defeat of the enemy fleet and the end of the invasion threat was tempered by grief at the loss of the nation's greatest hero. The battle of Trafalgar, one of the most decisive victories in naval history, was the beginning of a century of almost unrivaled dominance for the Royal Navy.

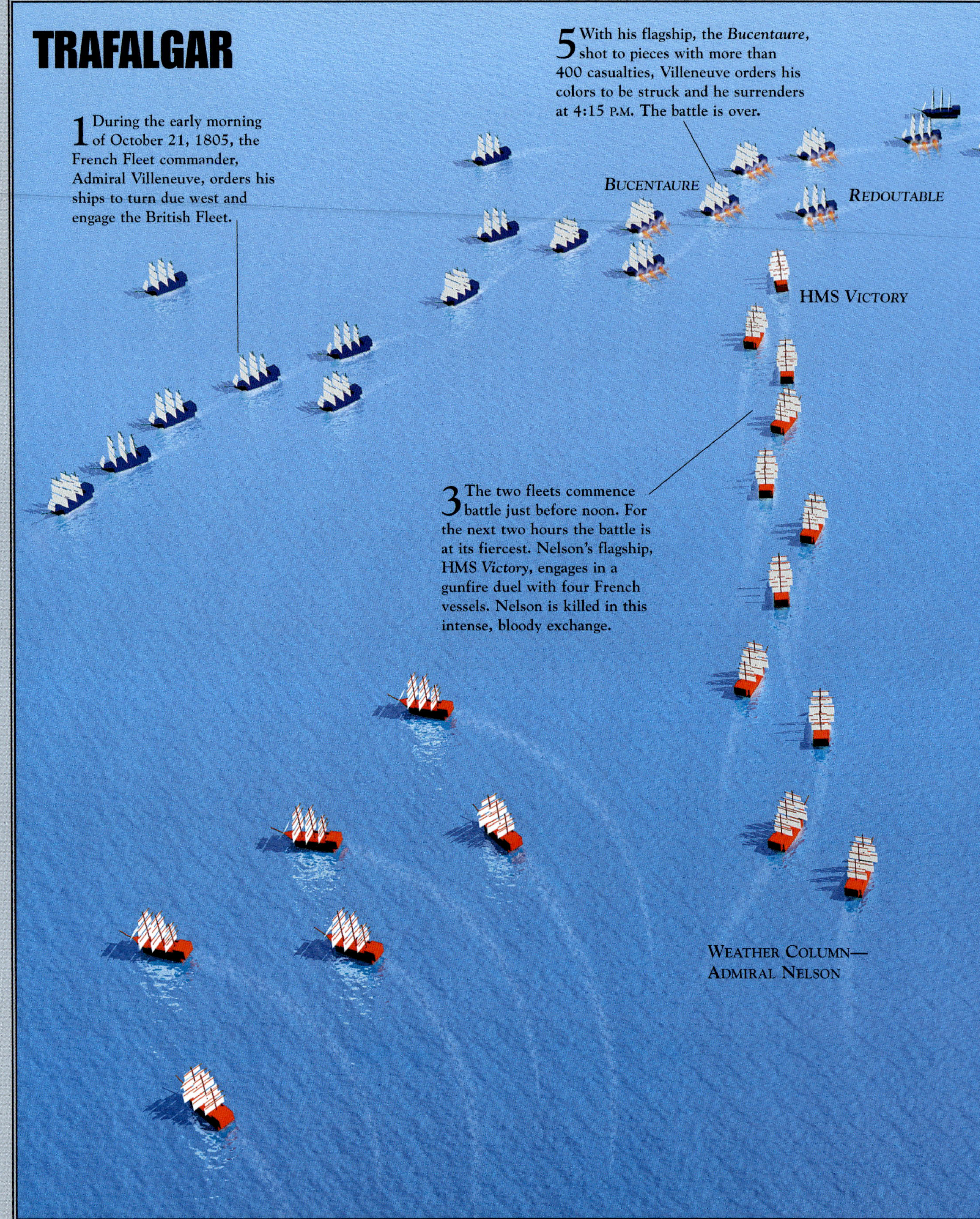
TRAFALGAR
1 During the early morning of October 21, 1805, the French Fleet commander, Admiral Villeneuve, orders his ships to turn due west and engage the British Fleet.
5 With his flagship, the Bucentaure, shot to pieces with more than 400 casualties, Villeneuve orders his colors to be struck and he surrenders at 4:15 P.M. The battle is over.
BUCENTAURE
REDOUTABLE
HMS VICTORY
3 The two fleets commence battle just before noon. For the next two hours the battle is at its fiercest. Nelson's flagship, HMS Victory, engages in a gunfire duel with four French vessels. Nelson is killed in this intense, bloody exchange.
WEATHER COLUMN—
ADMIRAL NELSON

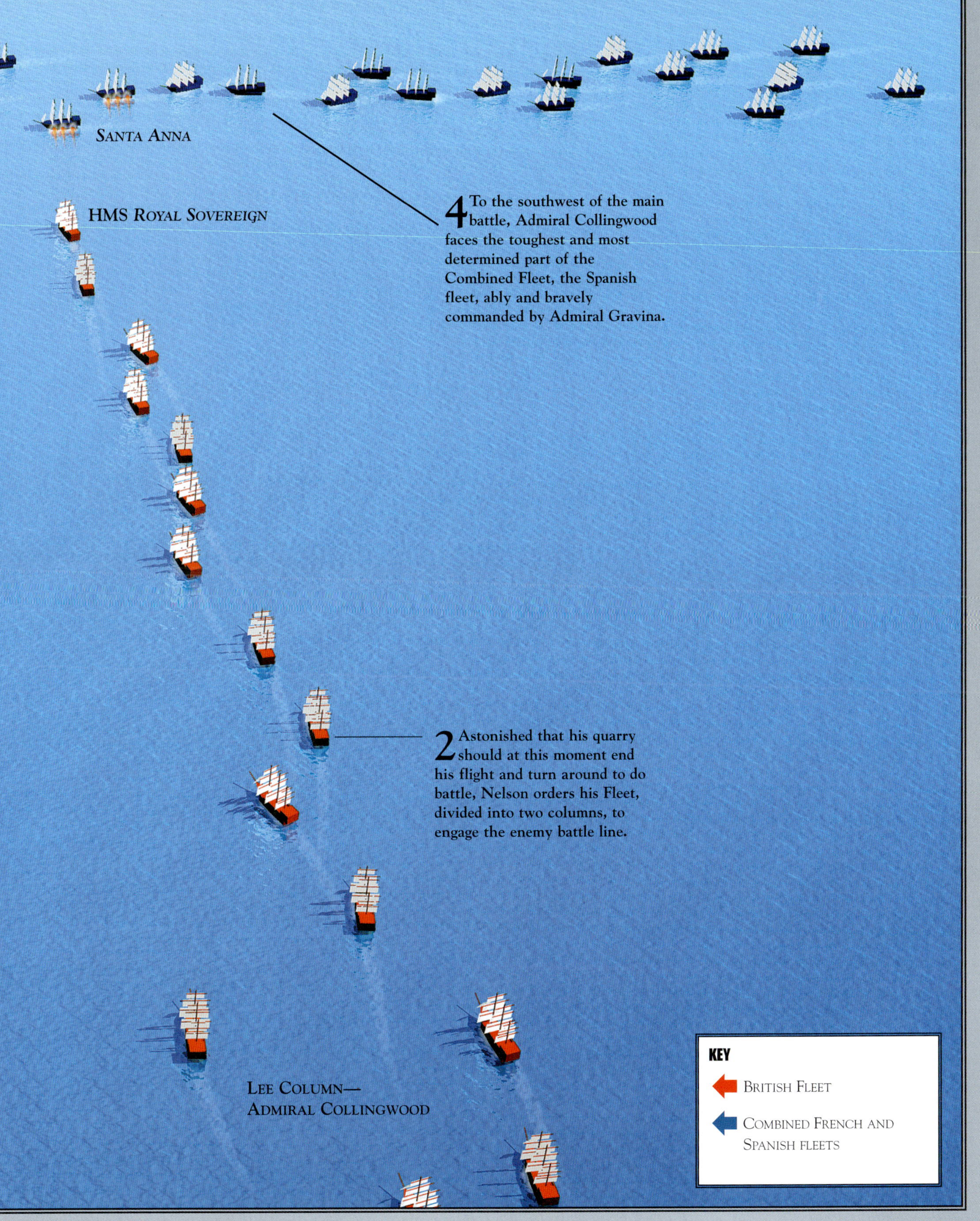
SANTA ANNA
HMS ROYAL SOVEREIGN
4 To the southwest of the main battle, Admiral Collingwood faces the toughest and most determined part of the Combined Fleet, the Spanish fleet, ably and bravely commanded by Admiral Gravina.
2 Astonished that his quarry should at this moment end his flight and turn around to do battle, Nelson orders his Fleet, divided into two columns, to engage the enemy battle line.
LEE COLUMN—
ADMIRAL COLLINGWOOD
KEY
BRITISH FLEET
COMBINED FRENCH AND SPANISH FLEETS

WATERLOO 1815

The final battle of the Napoleonic Wars saw the French Emperor's ambitions crushed once and for all. Despite flashes of his former brilliance in the campaign, Napoleon was unable to break up the Allied armies, and his fate was sealed by the Prussians marching to Wellington's aid on June 18 rather than falling back after their reverse at Ligny.

Revolutionary, then Napoleonic, France had been fighting Britain and her allies for 20 years when, finally, Napoleon abdicated in April 1814 and was exiled to the island of Elba. But discontent in France with the Bourbon King, Louis XVIII, led to Napoleon risking a passage from the island with 1,000 men for France, where he landed on March 1, 1815. Louis was forced to flee to Belgium while the Allies began to mobilize their armies. Napoleon sincerely wished for peace but the other European powers could never permit him to threaten peace again and he was therefore obliged to mobilize eight corps. Tired of war and bloodshed the French were reluctant to pay taxes and place recruits at the Emperor's disposal. The troops were

WATERLOO FACTS

Who: The Emperor Napoleon (1769–1821) with 72,000 men of the French Armée du Nord attacked an Anglo-Netherlandish army of 60,000 men under the Duke of Wellington (1769–1852), who was joined by Prince Gebhard von Blücher's Prussian army that evening.

What: In a superb defensive battle, Wellington's army was able, with great difficulty, to hold off Napoleon's disjointed attacks until the Prussian army arrived.

Where: The ridge of Mont St. Jean, near the village of Waterloo, 10 miles (16km) south of Brussels in Belgium.

When: June 18, 1815.

Why: Napoleon's escape from Elba and restoration of the Empire could not be tolerated by the Allies, who sought to crush this threat to European peace.

Outcome: Defeat at Waterloo forced Napoleon's second abdication, after which he was finally exiled to St. Helena in the South Atlantic.

Left: A classical painting of Marshal Ney's cuirassiers with foaming horses and waving black plumes riding with death-defying courage against the indomitable squares of British red-coated infantry.

weary as were the officers and even Napoleon's own marshals—most of whom owed their rank and wealth to his patronage—were reluctant to fight. This was especially true of Ney who disliked Napoleon as a tyrant who would plunge France into new and dangerous adventures. Ney, who had first promised Louis to bring back Napoleon in an iron cage before going over to him, felt deep down that Napoleon was a spent force and that France, facing a hostile European coalition, could not prevail. Unfortunately for Napoleon his irreplaceable Chief of Staff from the old days, Marshal Berthier, had died in an accident and his replacement Marshal Soult was not so talented. The combination of Napoleon's physical and mental decline, coupled with the bungling of his subordinates Soult and Ney would lead to defeat at Waterloo.

THE ALLIED ARMIES

On the opposite side Wellington was not having a smooth run either. His Peninsular veterans were dispersed across the world or had been demobilized. As a consequence Wellington was reduced to fighting Napoleon with a motley army of Dutch, Belgian, German mercenaries (Hessians and Nassauers), and a small force of British troops—many of whom were raw recruits. He had 68,800 infantry and 14,500 cavalry making a grand total of 92,300 troops divided into three infantry corps commanded by himself, General Hill, and the Dutch Prince of Orange. The cavalry was under the command of the Earl of Uxbridge who doubled as Wellington's second-in-command. Relations between the two men were frosty—Uxbridge had eloped with Wellington's sister-in-law—and had been appointed against Wellington's express wishes.

The Allies were therefore relying on the Prussians with 130,000 men to stem Napoleon. Their legendary commander, Field Marshal Prince Gebhard von Blücher (1742–1819) may never have been the greatest of strategists given his troops' nickname for him—Alte Forwärts ("Old Forwards"), but he could be relied upon to fight the French and come to the aid of Wellington who expected Napoleon to attempt to drive a wedge between their separate armies.

95TH RIFLES

In the British Army and the British expeditionary army in Belgium of 1815, the 95th Rifles stood out for two glaringly simple reasons. Firstly, its infantrymen were equipped with rifles, rather than the rest of the Army's trusted Brown Bess muskets. Secondly, when the rest of the army, irrespective of arm, wore the King's vivid scarlet uniforms the 95th clothed, for reason of camouflage, in dark-hued green. They were formed during the Peninsula War (1808–14) for a dual purpose—to fight as regular infantry and also as skirmishers and snipers ahead of the main army.

QUATRE BRAS AND LIGNY

On June 15 Napoleon crossed the frontier into Belgium with 123,000 men in his Armée du Nord at Charleroi—exactly where Wellington had not expected him to strike. "Napoleon has humbugged me, by God," was Wellington's comment as he rushed to assist his troops holding Marshal Ney at the crossroads of Quatre Bras. Ney had showed uncharacteristic lethargy by failing to occupy this vital position, compounding this error by only opening the battle in the afternoon and then using 4,000 cuirassiers to charge the British infantry squares. Obviously Ney had, three days later at Waterloo, a complete loss of memory as he repeated that mistake—charging unbroken infantry formations without infantry support.

That same day, June 16, the main battle took place at Ligny between Napoleon's main army of 71,000 men and Blücher's 84,000 Prussians. The Prussians had chosen to overextend themselves across marshy ground but Napoleon was not at his tactical best either. He delayed the battle until the afternoon when he was obliged to simply sledgehammer the Prussian lines into submission. For almost two hours savage fighting went on, often hand-to-hand with bayonets and firing at point-blank range. Prussian losses amounted to 19,000 and while Blücher quit the field Napoleon had sustained heavy losses—some 14,000 men—that he could ill afford. Napoleon sent Marshal Grouchy in pursuit of the Prussians with 30,000 men, but Grouchy failed to press the enemy closely, and far from retreating back to Germany as Napoleon had expected, Blücher marched west to support Wellington as he had promised.

Having beaten the Prussians Napoleon rushed to Quatre Bras where he found the British, having held off Ney's attacks, withdrawing from the battlefield in an orderly fashion, without any effort on the part of the French to pursue or harass them. Ney and his staff were sitting down for supper instead. Napoleon could not believe his eyes and gave his officers a violent dressing down that while it was deserved did nothing to raise Ney's morale. Fatally, Ney would remember this latest humiliation at Waterloo and acting upon his own initiative show that he was as dynamic as ever.

MONT ST. JEAN

There was a much-needed lull the following day as Wellington's army, numbering 74,300 troops in total, took up position around the farm of Mont St. Jean and the village of Waterloo where Wellington set up his headquarters. Wellington faced a French army of 74,500 men that had set up camp south of the road to Brussels while Napoleon, in spite of his superstitious frame of mind, had set up his headquarters at the inn of "La Belle Alliance."

The two armies may have been almost exactly and evenly matched numerically. This, however, took no account of the vitally qualitative differences between the two armies. Napoleon's troops were seasoned veterans, whereas most of Wellington's men were recently recruited troops and only 28,000 of these were British—they too in great part newly recruited men. Furthermore the French had not only more cavalry and artillery but what they had were of far greater quality than Wellington's. Not only did the French 12-pounder have a superior range to the British 9-pounder but the crews handling them were more experienced and better led. Perhaps this was due to the simple fact that Napoleon, now an emperor, had once been a young artillery officer whose handling of the French guns at Toulon in 1793 had, quite literally, shot him to fame? Wellington was, by contrast, an infantry commander.

DISPOSITIONS

As battlefields go, that of Waterloo, compared to Borodino (1812) in Russia, was a very compact and dense one where there was to be a lot of action in a compressed space in the course of a single day. That day, June 18, was to change the course of European history forever.

Wellington had drawn up his army based on divisions divided into three corps. His extreme left flank was secured by the German division of the Prince of Saxe-Weimar backed by Uxbridge's cavalry to their rear. On the opposite side—on the extreme right—was the Prince of Orange's Dutch-Belgian division; then came Clinton's division (behind the Braine l'Allend road); Cooke's division, at the junction of the Brussels road; Alten's division (facing the farm of La Haie) with Wellington's Reserve Corps and finally, strung out along the Ohain road, General Picton's

ABOVE: ON THE LEFT A BROODING, slouched Napoleon contrasts in a second oil painting with the determined look and fit frame of Wellington. The reality was that they were two of the best generals of their era, both determined to win.

RIGHT: IN THEIR CHARACTERISTIC bearskin caps, florid whiskers, and sideburns, the veterans of the Old Guard was Napoleon's last reserve—one that he threw away at Waterloo.

LEFT: THIS WELL EQUIPPED British private belonged to Wellington's finest infantry unit, the elite Coldstream Guards, who fought hard to hold the farm house of Hougoumont.

division—the finest, with Clinton's, in the whole Allied army. Napoleon's army was strung out along a parallel line to that of Wellington's perpendicular to the Charleroi to Brussels road with the left flank at the Nivelles road. Piré's cavalry was on the extreme left with Kellerman's III Cavalry Corps and the Cavalry of the Guard under Guyot at the rear, while Prince Jérôme Bonaparte's infantry faced the walled estate of Hougoumont. The center was made up of the divisions of General Count J.B. d'Erlon's I Corps with Milhaud's cavalry at the rear. The right flank was anchored on the position of La Haie.

Facing the prospect that Blücher might intervene at any moment, Napoleon had to make the first move and secure a swift and decisive victory over Wellington before he had to turn and face the Prussians. Should the two enemy armies actually link up it would spell doom for not only his army but his restored Empire as well. Everything depended upon this roll of the iron dice of war. Interestingly enough Napoleon's plan, as at Borodino in 1812, was unimaginative and depended upon using brute force in a frontal assault instead of trying to outflank or outmaneuver the Allied army. Napoleon aimed simply to break Wellington's line through the farm of La Haie Sainte in the center and occupy the crossroads behind, drive on and occupy Mont St. Jean farm.

THE BATTLE BEGINS

Napoleon had prepared to attack at 10:30 A.M. but there had been a downpour overnight that made the ground too soft for cavalry and artillery fire. The main assault was postponed, with fatal consequences, until 1 P.M. and the French began a preliminary artillery bombardment at 10:50 A.M. against the chateau of Hougoumont on Wellington's right held by the tough Hanoverian troops of the King's German Legion (KGL) and a detachment of Nassau troops.

To draw away Wellington's attention from his left flank—where Napoleon's main attack would be launched—Napoleon gave orders that his brother Prince Jérôme was to attack Hougoumont to draw off Wellington's reserves. But instead the Prince sent wave after wave of his infantry against the staunchly defended estate with little to show for it, tying down his own troops while Wellington only sent minimal reinforcements. He threw in all his four regiments and half of Foy's division for good measure. It was vital for Wellington to hold this crucial pivot point in the battle line at all costs, so he committed his toughest troops—the Scots and Coldstream Guards—to support the German defenders.

At one in the afternoon, as Napoleon prepared to attack, came unwelcome news with a courier that General Bülow's Prussian Corps (30,000 men) was approaching from the direction of Wavre. A cautious man would have withdrawn but Napoleon gambled on Grouchy, supposedly on his way to the battlefield, taking an hour to reach him and intercept the Prussians—it took four, and by that time the Prussians had helped Wellington beat Napoleon. As an additional insurance against the Prussians turning up, Napoleon ordered Count Lobau with 20,000 men to his right flank, facing east and the Prussians. Although a sensible move it also ensured that the main assault against Wellington was considerably weakened.

D'ERLON'S ATTACK

At 1:30 P.M. some 84 guns positioned at La Belle Alliance opened fire for the next half hour. These French 12-pound guns could fire roundshot some 1.1 miles (1.8km). Because of the soft, wet ground this fire proved ineffective as the shot hit the ground and sank into it, instead of ricocheting through the Allied infantry. Even if they had, Wellington had placed most of his precious troops—that he wished to spare—just beyond the ridge rather than on top of it. It was not until 2 P.M.—and every hour was precious for Napoleon before the

BELOW: A BAKER RIFLE AND BAYONET, as used by rifle regiments—such as the 95th Rifles—in the Hundred Days' War. First produced in 1800, the Baker rifle was the first standard-issue, British-made rifle accepted for the British armed forces.

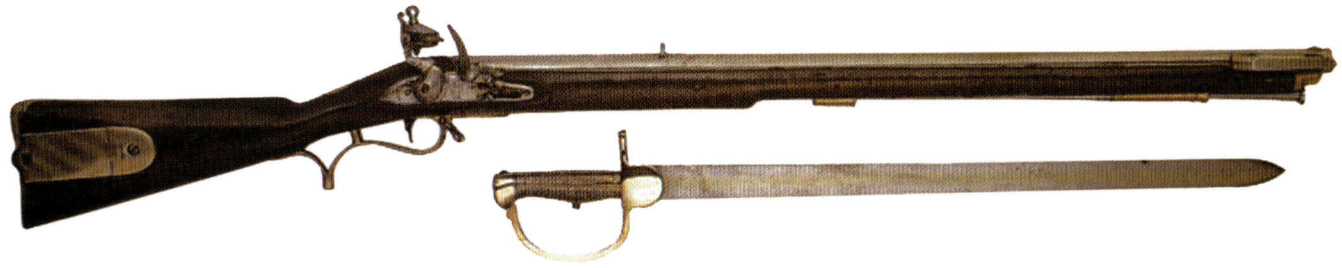

Prussians arrived—that Napoleon unleashed d'Erlon's I Corps. D'Erlon, hoping to break through the Allied lines by sheer weight of numbers, formed his divisions into three massive columns of battalions deployed one behind the other. Although very vulnerable to Allied artillery and musket fire in this formation, the avalanche of blue-clad infantry proved almost irresistible once I Corps' assault got underway sweeping van Biljandt's exposed 1st Netherland (Dutch-Belgian) Brigade aside. Wellington's left-center position buckled under this huge wave of attacking infantry forcing him to commit all the units he could spare. The best he had was Sir Thomas Picton's 5th Infantry Divison (6,745 men) made up of British (8th and 9th Brigades) and Hanoverian troops (5th Brigade).

Picton's ferocious counterattacks, backed by Uxbridge's cavalry, including Sir William Ponsonby's 2nd (Union) Brigade, held the French—only just though and only at an enormous coast. Both Picton and Ponsonby died, Uxbridge lost a leg from a cannon shot while some 40 per cent of his men were either dead, captured, or wounded. But their sacrifices were worth it since the French attack ground to a halt. They began to retreat, finally fleeing, leaving some 3,000 prisoners for the British to pick up. An hour later (by 3 P.M.) the British had defeated the first French assault.

NEY'S CAVALRY ATTACKS

At 3:30 P.M. Napoleon ordered his artillery to pound La Haie Sainte and for Ney to prepare for a new assault that he would lead in person. But without informing Napoleon Ney ordered 5,000 of his cavalry to attack what he thought were retreating enemy troops, but Wellington was simply bringing some of his units out of the range of fire and redeploying the rest. Lacking infantry or artillery support, Ney's cavalry stormed in the finest French style of mad bravado up the slope to be met by a hail of artillery and massed musket fire at point-blank range. Hundreds of cavalrymen met their death with extreme courage while the British infantry (formed in squares for defence) repelled wave after wave of the cuirassiers, dragoons, and lancers coming at them.

Ney retreated, reformed, and charged again, and again without breaking the British. At 5 P.M. General François Kellerman joined the attack with his III Cavalry Corps. Neither Ney nor Kellerman had thought of getting Napoleon's permission before they set after the "retreating" Allied troops. The intensity of the fighting was such that Ney had four horses shot from underneath him while some of the British squares were close to breaking point after Kellerman joined in. Yet it all proved to be in vain and by 6 P.M. even Ney had had enough and simply walked back, his last horse having been shot, to the French lines.

Napoleon could not believe what Ney had done or that Wellington's "mongrel" troops had been able to stand up to this onslaught. To atone for his rash stupidity Ney did eventually take La Haie Sainte held to the last by the KGL. Having lost the 2nd Regiment and its commander, Baron Ompteda, they had had enough and retreated with the broken 1st Hanoverian Brigade. Wellington's center was in a state of near collapse, which threatened to undo his entire army.

THE FINAL ATTACK

The Prussians had begun to appear at the edge of the battlefield (the Bois de Paris) by 4 P.M. and an hour later Napoleon was forced to shore up Lobau's VI Corps—now reduced to only 7,000 men—by sending 4,000 men of the Young Guard. By 7 P.M. von Zeithen's I Corps had arrived to back up Bülow's men. In a last attempt to break through Wellington's center Napoleon ordered the Old Guard—his final reserve and troops who had never been beaten—to attack in two columns, 75 men abreast.

Yet again, British troops concealed behind the ridge were able to surprise the columns before they could deploy into line and shattered them with close-range musketry. As the Old Guard fell back, the French army's morale finally cracked and they broke and fled, shouting "Sauve qui peut!"—"Every man for himself!" and "Trahison!"—"Treachery!" Napoleon fled in a coach and at 8:30 P.M. Wellington met his savior Blücher at La Belle Alliance.

AFTERMATH

The French had lost some 30,000 men. Wellington had lost 15,000 and the Prussians 6,700. By 5 A.M. the following day Napoleon was back at Charleroi heading toward Paris. On June 22, he abdicated for a second time, fled Paris, and on July 15 boarded HMS *Bellerophon* at Plymouth. Exactly four months later he stepped ashore on the island of St. Helena, his "home" until his death.

RIGHT: THE FINEST and noblest of the British cavalry, the Scots Greys, launched their legendary attack against the artillery and infantry of the French center with catastrophic results.

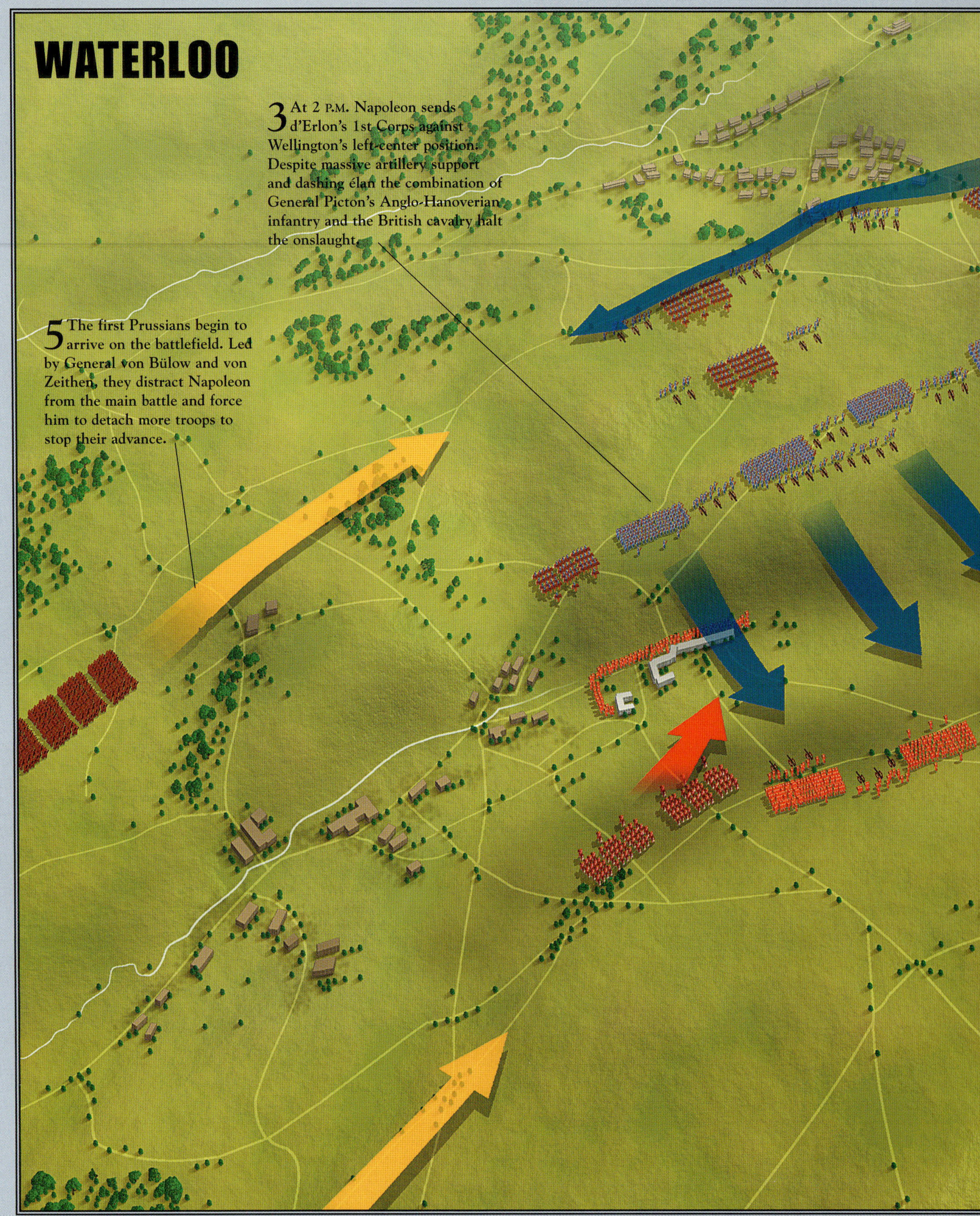
WATERLOO
3 At 2 P.M. Napoleon sends d'Erlon's 1st Corps against Wellington's left-center position. Despite massive artillery support and dashing élan the combination of General Picton's Anglo-Hanoverian infantry and the British cavalry halt the onslaught.
5 The first Prussians begin to arrive on the battlefield. Led by General von Bülow and von Zeithen, they distract Napoleon from the main battle and force him to detach more troops to stop their advance.

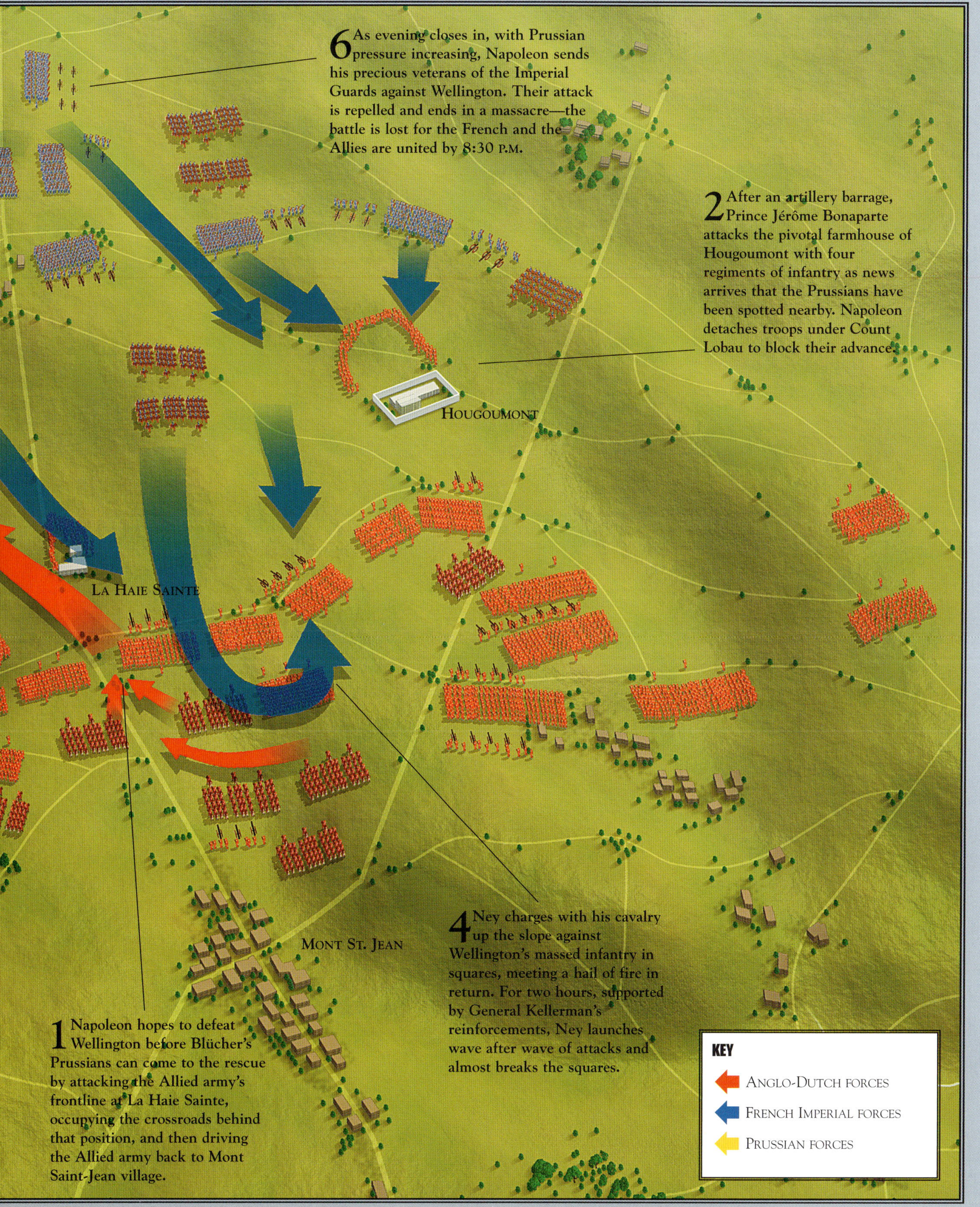
6 As evening closes in, with Prussian pressure increasing, Napoleon sends his precious veterans of the Imperial Guards against Wellington. Their attack is repelled and ends in a massacre—the battle is lost for the French and the Allies are united by 8:30 P.M.
2 After an artillery barrage, Prince Jérôme Bonaparte attacks the pivotal farmhouse of Hougoumont with four regiments of infantry as news arrives that the Prussians have been spotted nearby. Napoleon detaches troops under Count Lobau to block their advance.
Hougoumont
La Haie Sainte
Mont St. Jean
4 Ney charges with his cavalry up the slope against Wellington's massed infantry in squares, meeting a hail of fire in return. For two hours, supported by General Kellerman's reinforcements, Ney launches wave after wave of attacks and almost breaks the squares.
1 Napoleon hopes to defeat Wellington before Blücher's Prussians can come to the rescue by attacking the Allied army's frontline at La Haie Sainte, occupying the crossroads behind that position, and then driving the Allied army back to Mont Saint-Jean village.
KEY
Anglo-Dutch forces
French Imperial forces
Prussian forces

US

GETTYSBURG 1863

In an epic three-day battle, the brief history of the Confederacy reached its zenith as General Robert E. Lee's second invasion of the North was repulsed in southern Pennsylvania. After Gettysburg, the outcome of the American Civil War appeared inevitable as Union armies maintained an offensive posture on all fronts.

For General Robert E. Lee, the stunning Confederate victory at Chancellorsville in May 1863, provided both his crowning achievement and his darkest moment of battlefield command. Although the Union army under General Joseph Hooker had been routed, Lee's most capable lieutenant, General Thomas J. "Stonewall" Jackson, had been mortally wounded by friendly fire. Although the loss of Jackson was a severe blow, Lee nevertheless felt compelled to follow up the victory at Chancellorsville. He reorganized the Army of Northern Virginia into three corps, commanded by generals James Longstreet, A.P. Hill, and Richard S. Ewell. The Confederate army was flush with victory and stood at the height of its strength;

GETTYSBURG FACTS

Who: General Robert E. Lee (1807–70) and 75,000 soldiers of the Confederate Army of Northern Virginia opposed 97,000 troops of the Union Army of the Potomac, commanded by General George G. Meade (1815–72).

What: During three days of fighting, Confederate forces failed to penetrate Union defenses along a 3-mile (4.8km), fish-hook shaped line from Culp's Hill and Cemetery Hill southward along Cemetery Ridge to Little Round Top.

Where: South of the town of Gettysburg, in Southern Pennsylvania.

When: July 1–3, 1863.

Why: For the second time in the American Civil War, the Confederate Army launched an invasion of Northern territory.

Outcome: Lee's invasion was repulsed, and the military might of the Confederacy suffered irreplaceable losses in what was rapidly becoming a war of attrition. President Abraham Lincoln issued one of the enduring documents of American freedom with the Gettysburg Address.

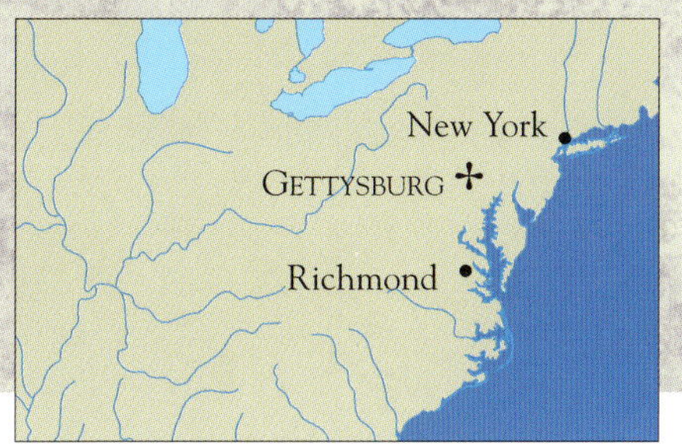

LEFT: IN THIS SECTION OF THE GETTYSBURG CYCLORAMA, painted in 1883 by French artist Paul Philippoteaux, the 19th Massachusetts and 42nd New York regiments rush forward to bolster the Union line at the height of Pickett's Charge. During the high tide of Confederate military strength, a handful of the attackers breached the Union position on Cemetery Ridge, but only briefly.

LEFT: A CONFEDERATE INFANTRYMAN of the 1st Texas Brigade lunges forward with his bayonet-tipped musket. Troops of the 1st Texas were heavily engaged in the capture of Devil's Den on July 2, 1863.

therefore, its commander looked to the north for a second time. Lee's aims were similar to those that had precipitated the invasion of the North, which had ended nine months earlier with the battle of Antietam. Destroying the Pennsylvania Railroad bridge over the Susquehanna River would disrupt enemy communications, and Confederate troops could sustain themselves with supplies procured from Northern farms. Lee might capture Harrisburg, the Pennsylvania state capital, and threaten Baltimore, Philadelphia, or Washington, D.C. Perhaps most important, the population of the North was becoming war-weary. The presence of victorious Confederate forces in Union territory might bring about peace overtures and secure Southern independence.

THE CAMPAIGN

On June 3, 1863, the Army of Northern Virginia began streaming steadily to the northwest, across the mountains of the Blue Ridge, and then northward through the Shenandoah Valley. For three weeks, the Confederates operated virtually at will against only token resistance. With Ewell's corps in the van, the Confederates were spread across miles of the Pennsylvania countryside. By the end of the month, Ewell was menacing Harrisburg, General Jubal Early's division had occupied the town of York, and Robert Rodes' division was miles to the north at Carlisle.

Hooker's Army of the Potomac became alerted to the Confederate offensive on June 25, during a heavy clash between Rebel cavalry under General J.E.B. Stuart and Federal horsemen commanded by General Alfred Pleasanton at Brandy Station, Virginia. Hooker set his army in motion to intercept the Confederates and requested that the arsenal at Harpers Ferry be abandoned and its garrison of 10,000 men added to the field army's ranks. When President Lincoln and the Union army's general-in-chief, Henry W. Halleck, declined, Hooker asked to be relieved of command. On June 28, a mere four days before the battle of Gettysburg, General George G. Meade was placed in command of the Army of the Potomac.

The rapid northward movement of the Union army caused Stuart to initiate a lengthy ride around Meade and out of contact with Lee. Thus, during a critical period of the campaign, the Confederate commander was deprived of his eyes and ears. Lee, warned by a Southern sympathizer, knew for certain only that the Army of the Potomac was on the march. Without intelligence from Stuart, he had no choice but to concentrate his forces. Reluctantly, Lee ordered Ewell to abandon his planned attack on Harrisburg and join the corps of Hill and Longstreet at Gettysburg.

IN SEARCH OF SHOES

On the morning of July 1, Lee was with Longstreet's Corps at Chambersburg, 25 miles (40km) west of Gettysburg. Hill's Corps was 8 miles (12.8km) west of Gettysburg at Cashtown. Neither Lee nor Meade intended to fight at Gettysburg, which held virtually no strategic value. Lee, in fact, had admonished his subordinate commanders not to bring on a general engagement until the army could be concentrated on favorable ground. Events, however, soon began to develop beyond the control of either senior commander.

Early had already passed through Gettysburg on June 26 during his division's march to York. He sent a note to Hill, informing him that a cache of shoes might be found in the town. Four days later, the leading division of Hill's corps, under General Henry Heth, reached Cashtown. Heth sent a brigade down the Chambersburg Pike to Gettysburg in

GENERAL GEORGE MEADE

General George Gordon Meade, a Pennsylvanian known for his volatile temper, commanded an effective defense at Gettysburg, holding critical high ground and utilizing interior lines. Criticized for not vigorously pursuing Lee into Virginia, Meade commanded the Army of the Potomac for the duration of the war but was subordinate to General in Chief Ulysses S. Grant, who traveled with the campaigning army. He died in Philadelphia in 1872.

search of the shoes. The brigade commander, General James Pettigrew, withdrew from the Gettysburg area when he spotted a large force of Union cavalry moving up from the south. On July 1, Hill ordered two full divisions, those of Heth and General Dorsey Pender, to Gettysburg to determine the strength of the Union force. Probing eastward, the Confederates found two brigades of General John Buford's cavalry, screening the advance of the left wing of the Army of the Potomac. Buford had ordered his troopers to dismount and take up defensive positions west of the town and waited for the Rebels to return.

The decisive battle of the American Civil War was taking shape while the bulk of both armies and both senior commanders were not present on the field. Buford's decision to stand and fight combined with Hill's decision to send a force much greater than necessary on a reconnaissance mission precipitated an engagement from which neither side could readily extricate itself.

RIGHT: SOLDIERS OF THE 114th Pennsylvania Zouaves, their colorful uniforms patterned after those of French military units, were heavily engaged with Confederate troops from Georgia and Mississippi at the Peach Orchard and the Wheatfield on July 2, 1863.

THE FIRST DAY

Buford's dismounted cavalrymen fought like lions against ever-increasing numbers of Confederate infantrymen. For two hours they stood firm, before infantry of General John F. Reynolds' I Corps rolled in from the south. As he urged the famed Iron Brigade forward, Reynolds was killed in the saddle by a Confederate sharpshooter. Both sides committed fresh troops to the fray, and the fighting intensified. Union troops from New York and Wisconsin captured more than 200 Rebel soldiers, who had been trapped in the cut of an unfinished railroad. Hard pressed, other Union troops fought desperately to prevent their left flank from being turned.

From about 4 miles (6.4km) away, Ewell and Rodes, on the march from Carlisle, could hear Hill's artillery firing. By now, elements of the Union XI Corps, under General Oliver O. Howard, were shuffling through the streets of Gettysburg toward the fighting. The Confederate generals, however, recognized an opportunity to hit the exposed Union right flank. Eventually, the combined weight of Rodes' assaults, the renewed effort of Heth's division, and advances by three of Pender's brigades threatened to overwhelm the Union I Corps on Seminary Ridge.

It was, however, the XI Corps on the Union right that gave way first. Raising a cloud of dust on the Harrisburg Road, Early's division appeared from the north and routed a Union division, which had taken up positions on a small knoll. Georgia, Louisiana, and North Carolina troops stunned the Union right, and successive units of the XI Corps faltered, broke, and ran through the town to the relative safety of Cemetery Hill.

Its flank fully exposed, the patchwork battle line of the Union I Corps on Seminary Ridge collapsed. Streaming back through Gettysburg, more and more Union troops reached Cemetery Hill, where General Winfield Scott Hancock, commander of the II Corps, had become the fifth general of the day to command the Union forces. Meade would not reach Gettysburg from Taneytown, Maryland until after midnight. Lee had arrived on the field at 1:30 P.M. but was largely a bystander during most of the fighting.

As the Union troops scrambled to consolidate their position on Cemetery Hill, Lee grasped the significance of his opportunity to win a decisive victory. He forwarded a

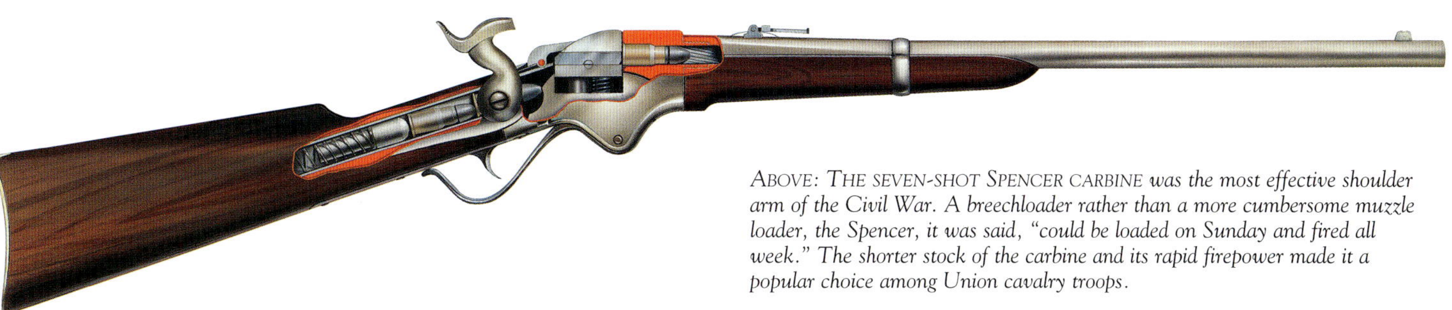

ABOVE: THE SEVEN-SHOT SPENCER CARBINE was the most effective shoulder arm of the Civil War. A breechloader rather than a more cumbersome muzzle loader, the Spencer, it was said, "could be loaded on Sunday and fired all week." The shorter stock of the carbine and its rapid firepower made it a popular choice among Union cavalry troops.

UNION CAVALRY OFFICER

His saber drawn, a Union cavalry officer leads a charge. Much maligned early in the war, Union cavalry units continued to improve, holding their own and eventually getting the better of the vaunted Confederate cavalry in several fights.

cryptic verbal order to Ewell, which said in effect that it was only necessary to "press those people" in order to take possession of the heights and to capture Cemetery Hill, nearby Culp's Hill or both "if practicable."

The fight, however, had gone out of Ewell. The enemy beyond Cemetery Hill was of undetermined strength. Hill's corps was spent. Longstreet would not reach Gettysburg for hours. Under protest from subordinates, Ewell declined to continue his attack. During the night, Union reinforcements continued to arrive, Culp's Hill was occupied in force, and a defensive line was established across Cemetery Ridge to Little Round Top. Ewell's decision remains, to this day, one of the most controversial of the Civil War.

THE SECOND DAY

In the early hours of July 2, both sides held councils of war. Meade determined to stand fast, although the entire Union army had not yet reached Gettysburg. Lee, against the advice of Longstreet, decided that an attack on the Union left combined with a renewed effort against Cemetery Hill and Culp's Hill might negate Meade's advantage of interior lines and roll up the entire Union position.

Longstreet took pains to conceal his march to his designated jump-off position and was not ready to attack until about 3:30 P.M. Confederate artillery fired on the positions of the exposed Union division commanded by General Daniel Sickles in the Peach Orchard as infantrymen from Alabama and Texas marched to the east and turned northward toward Little Round Top and a jumble of huge boulders known locally as Devil's Den. Major General Gouverneur K. Warren, the chief engineer of the Army of the Potomac, rode to the summit of Little Round Top as the Confederates massed for their assault. He recognized that if the Confederates captured this key hill an enfilading fire would render the entire Union line untenable. Warren searched frantically for troops to defend the position. His plea for help was answered by two brigades of General George Sykes' V Corps. These troops from Pennsylvania, New York, and Maine scrambled into position moments before the attacking Confederates started up the slope.

While the desperate defenders of Little Round Top, scavenging ammunition from their own dead and wounded, beat back multiple attacks, fighting raged nearby. Successive Confederate assaults shattered Sickles' salient in the Peach Orchard, and the Wheatfield became a scene of tremendous carnage. At the end of the day, Longstreet had overrun Devil's Den and his troops controlled the Peach Orchard. However, thanks to Warren's initiative, Little Round Top was in Union hands.

At Culp's Hill and Cemetery Hill, Ewell sent troops from the divisions of Early and General Edward Johnson forward in the fading light. Fighting continued for several hours as the Confederates made headway. Some of Early's troops reached the crest of Culp's Hill and engaged in hand-to-hand fighting with the defenders. While the rest of his line was unmolested, Hancock was able to reinforce the threatened area, and by 10 P.M. the fighting had petered out.

BELOW: PHOTOGRAPHER TIMOTHY O'SULLIVAN recorded this grisly scene of Union dead in a meadow near the Peach Orchard. These soldiers were probably killed on July 2, 1863, defending the advanced positions of the Union III Corps.

THE THIRD DAY

The climactic day at Gettysburg began on the Union right at Culp's Hill and Spangler's Spring, where Confederate forces still held earthworks dug by the Federals on the night of July 1. At daylight, further Confederate attacks against the strong entrenchments on Culp's Hill proved fruitless. Two Union divisions under Generals Thomas Ruger and John Geary rooted elements of Johnson's division out of their hard-won but meager lodgment. Before noon, the Federals had regained their lost earthworks, and the fighting had ebbed. A strange silence now hung over the field. It was a deceptive quiet, for the final act of the Gettysburg drama was to unfold in a few short hours.

Lee apparently reasoned that Meade had left his center vulnerable to attack by reinforcing his flanks. Therefore, a concentrated blow against the Union centre on Cemetery Ridge might break through the line. Longstreet strongly dissented. The attacking troops would be obliged to cross more than a mile of open ground and traverse a picket fence along the Emmitsburg Road, all the while exposed to artillery fire from massed guns on Cemetery Ridge and the heights at either end of the Union line.

Most of Lee's army had been heavily engaged on July 2, and the only substantial force available to mount such an assault was the division of General George Pickett, which had guarded Confederate supply wagons for the previous two days. Pickett commanded three brigades, led by generals Richard B. Garnett, James L. Kemper, and Lewis A. Armistead. These would be supported by the divisions of Joseph Pettigrew and Isaac Trimble, who had assumed command for the wounded Heth and Pender respectively. The attacking force would number roughly 15,000 men.

At 1 P.M., nearly 150 Confederate guns opened a cannonade against the Union center. Soon, approximately 80 Union cannon replied from Cemetery Ridge. The artillery duel continued for two hours. Then, at 3 P.M., Pickett shouted, "Up men and to your posts! Don't forget today that you are from Old Virginia!"

Pickett's troops stepped off to the northeast, wheeled with parade-ground precision to the east, and headed toward the Union center. Their objective was a large copse of trees on the crest of Cemetery Ridge. As they crossed the open fields, Union artillery began to tear large gaps in the Confederate ranks. Then, as the Rebels came closer, Union infantry opened fire from the low stone wall to the front of the charging mass and against both of its flanks. Following the battle, the sharp 90-degree angle of the wall came to be known simply as The Angle.

Garnett was killed, and General Kemper fell seriously wounded. On foot, Armistead led his men through a momentary breach in the Union line, waving his hat perched atop his sword. As he lay his hand on a Union cannon, Armistead was mortally wounded. No Confederate reinforcements were available to exploit the breakthrough, and Union troops steadily closed on both flanks. At long last, the shattered remnants of the famous Pickett's Charge limped back toward their own lines, having achieved nothing but immortality. The high tide of the Confederacy had smashed itself upon the rock of the Union center.

AFTERMATH

On July 4, Lee began a long, painful retreat to Virginia, his dream of a military victory on Northern soil dashed. That same day, the Confederate city of Vicksburg, Mississippi, surrendered, and the South was split in two. These devastating defeats sealed the fate of the Confederacy. In the three-day orgy of death and destruction at Gettysburg, the Union suffered 3,149 killed and 19,664 wounded or captured. The Confederacy suffered 4,536 dead and 18,089 wounded or taken prisoner. On November 19, 1863, President Lincoln offered a short speech of slightly more than 200 words during the dedication of a new cemetery for the Union soldiers killed at Gettysburg. The Gettysburg Address still resonates more than two centuries later.

BELOW: *In one of the few photographs taken during the dedication of the Gettysburg National Cemetery on November 19, 1863, President Abraham Lincoln is barely visible seated at the left on the crowded speaker's platform. Lincoln's Gettysburg Address, consisting of slightly more than 200 words, remains one of the principal documents of American freedom.*

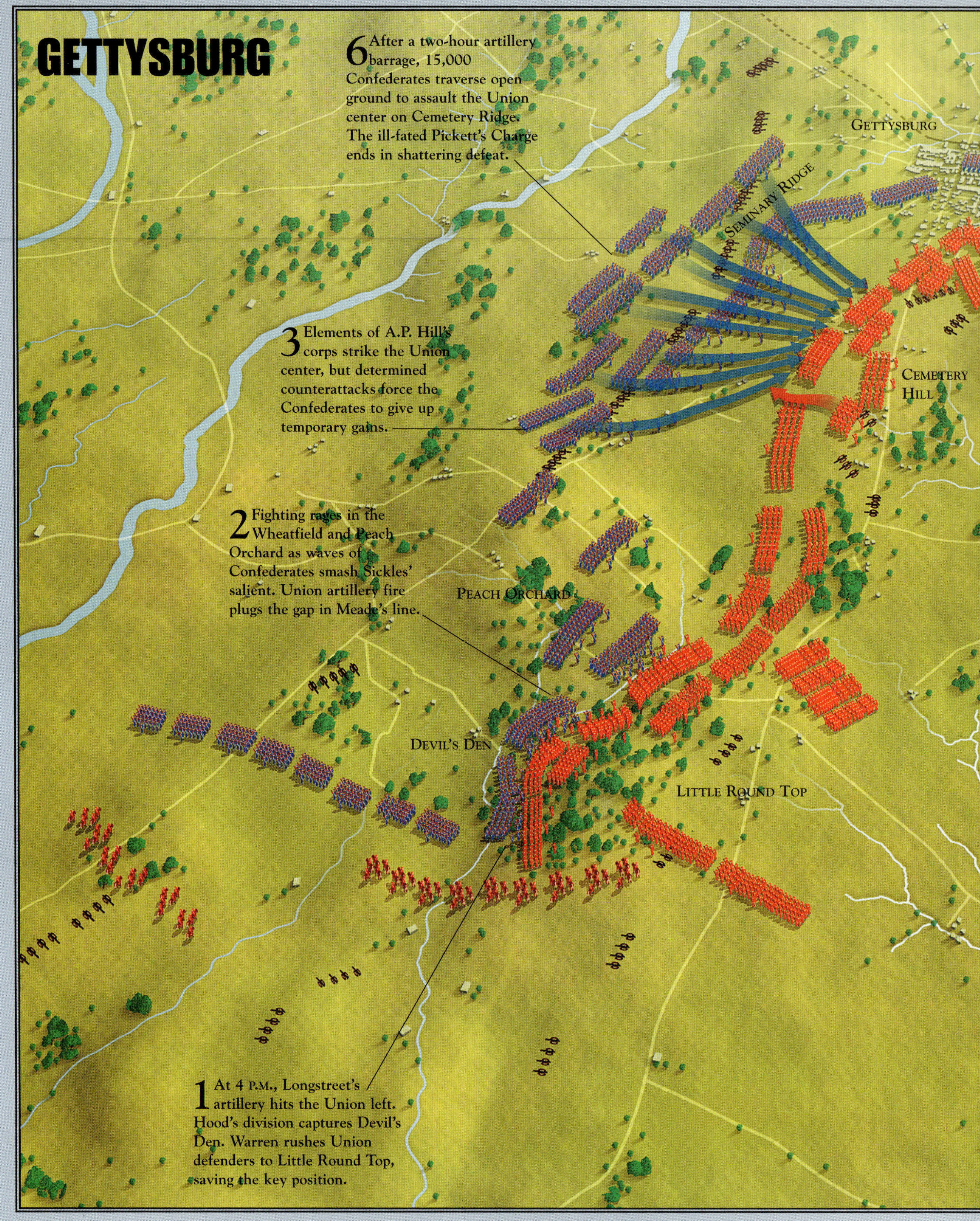
GETTYSBURG
6 After a two-hour artillery barrage, 15,000 Confederates traverse open ground to assault the Union center on Cemetery Ridge. The ill-fated Pickett's Charge ends in shattering defeat.
GETTYSBURG
SEMINARY RIDGE
CEMETERY HILL
3 Elements of A.P. Hill's corps strike the Union center, but determined counterattacks force the Confederates to give up temporary gains.
2 Fighting rages in the Wheatfield and Peach Orchard as waves of Confederates smash Sickles' salient. Union artillery fire plugs the gap in Meade's line.
PEACH ORCHARD
DEVIL'S DEN
LITTLE ROUND TOP
1 At 4 P.M., Longstreet's artillery hits the Union left. Hood's division captures Devil's Den. Warren rushes Union defenders to Little Round Top, saving the key position.

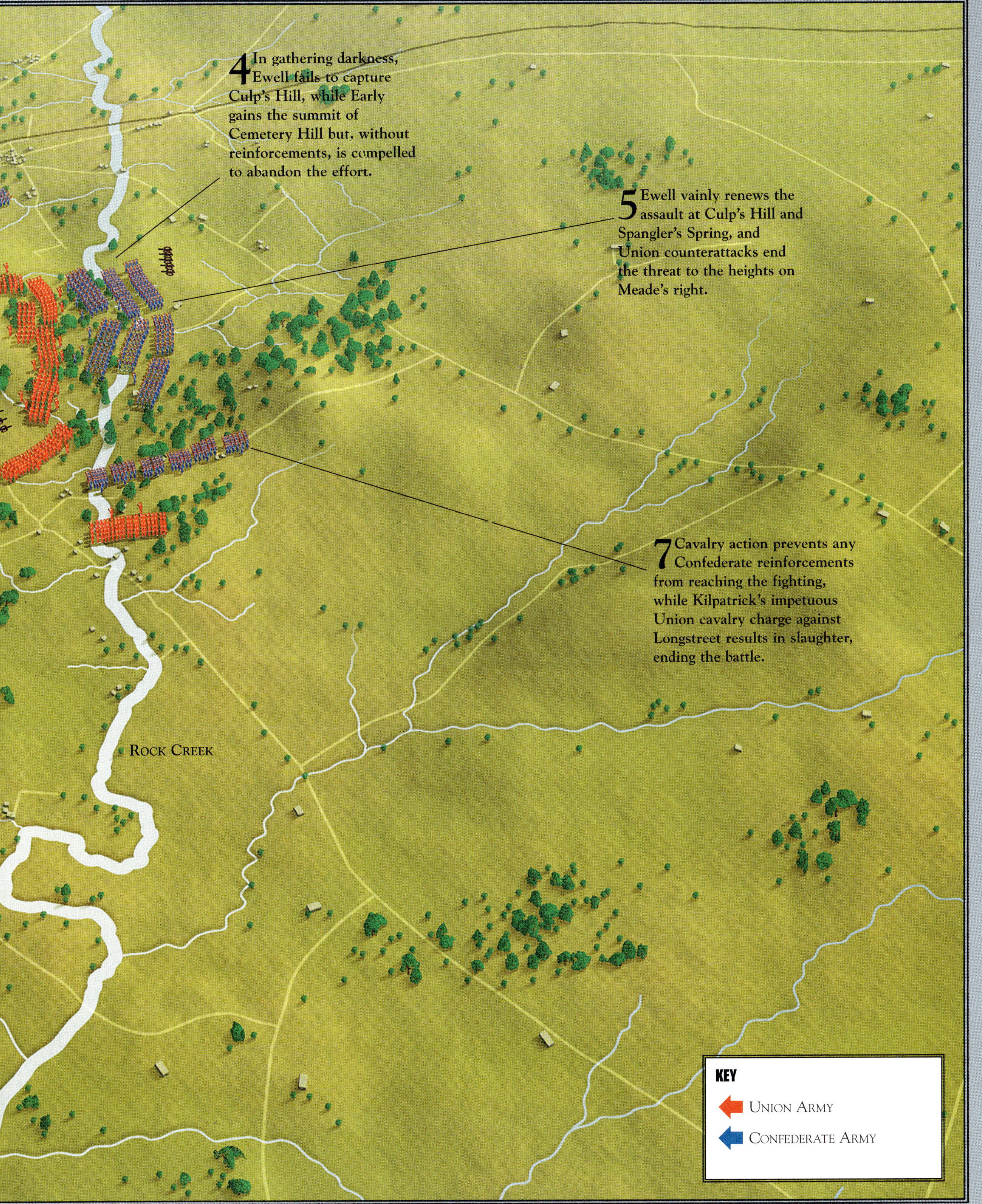
4 In gathering darkness, Ewell fails to capture Culp's Hill, while Early gains the summit of Cemetery Hill but, without reinforcements, is compelled to abandon the effort.
5 Ewell vainly renews the assault at Culp's Hill and Spangler's Spring, and Union counterattacks end the threat to the heights on Meade's right.
7 Cavalry action prevents any Confederate reinforcements from reaching the fighting, while Kilpatrick's impetuous Union cavalry charge against Longstreet results in slaughter, ending the battle.
Rock Creek
KEY
Union Army
Confederate Army

VERDUN 1916

Verdun epitomizes the attritional struggle that became characteristic of World War I on the Western Front. Intended to destroy the French reserves, the battle drew in massive numbers of German troops as well, and ended without any decisive result.

As World War I settled down into trench warfare in late 1914, it became more or less impossible to inflict a traditional victory on the enemy. Previously, victory was decided by the defeat of an army in the field or the occupation (or threat of occupation) of key areas such as capital cities. That was simply impossible now. There seemed to be no way to break through the lines and capture strategic objectives, and deep defensive positions made it virtually impossible to drive the enemy from the field. The problem in both cases was the availability of reserves, coupled with the capability to move them to a threatened point faster than a successful attack could be exploited.

Victory in the Great War would therefore be a matter of exhausting the other side, of making the cost of continuing so high that peace became essential, at

VERDUN FACTS

Who: French Second Army under General Henri Pétain (1856–1951), later replaced by General Robert Nivelle (1856–1924), versus the German Fifth Army under Crown Prince Wilhelm (1882–1951), with General Erich von Falkenhayn (1861–1922) with overall responsibility for operations as Chief of the General Staff.

What: The fortified city of Verdun was besieged and the attackers slowly ground their way in while artillery inflicted horrendous casualties. A counteroffensive eventually regained the lost ground.

Where: The city of Verdun on the Meuse River, France.

When: February 21 to December 18, 1916.

Why: The German high command wanted to draw French reserves into a "meatgrinder" and destroy them, forcing France to make peace.

Outcome: After a hideous attritional struggle all that was achieved was massive casualties on both sides.

LEFT: FRENCH INFANTRY ADVANCE *through the shattered landscape, surrounded by the horrors of war. There is still something splendid about images of this kind—the reality was infinitely more dreary and squalid.*

LEFT: A FRENCH 1897-VINTAGE cannon. Designed for mobile operations in the open, weapons of this sort were less useful in the static trench warfare on the Western Front than high-trajectory howitzers and mortars.

whatever price. The key here, once again, was reserves. So long as the opposition had sufficient manpower available to feed into the combat zone, the war could go on. The German high command therefore came up with a plan to destroy the French reserves by drawing them into a "meatgrinder." The German plan was to attack something that the French had to defend, and to destroy their army with artillery and infantry attacks. The chosen objective was the fortified city of Verdun.

VERDUN

Verdun was an ideal target in many ways. Lying in a loop of the Meuse River, the city had poor communications. Only one road ran in and out of the city. The logistic problems of the attack were eased by the fact that there was a major German railhead just 12 miles (19.3km) away, allowing quick transportation of ammunition, supplies, and reinforcements as the attack developed. Verdun lay in a relatively quiet sector of the front, and many of the heavy guns of its forts had been sent to other sectors where they seemed to be more badly needed. It was garrisoned by three divisions, which represented fairly light defenses.

German offensive plans included the assembly of 10 divisions to make the actual attack, supported by experimental "infantry batteries" of 3in (77mm) field guns, which were supposed to advance with the infantry to provide direct support but in the event were unable to cross the shell-torn wasteland. Another new weapon also made its debut at Verdun: the flamethrower. The attack was supported by large quantities of heavy guns—more than 1,400 pieces in total. These included huge 16.5in (420mm) and 12in (305mm) weapons that had previously been used to reduce forts in Belgium. More than 500 minenwerfer were also deployed. These fired a 100lb (45.3kg) explosive shell, which could have a deadly effect if it landed in a trench. Countless lighter weapons such as trench mortars were also available.

The offensive was codenamed Operation Gericht ("Judgment"). Its aim was to force the French into a battle of attrition on unequal terms. If they failed to meet the challenge, Verdun would fall. If they stood and fought, their army would be bled white and they would ultimately be forced to sue for peace. The operation was scheduled to start on February 10, but was delayed by bad weather until the 21st. Although the preparations for the operation were spotted, there was no attempt to reinforce Verdun, and the initial artillery onslaught caught the garrison unprepared.

OPENING BARRAGE

As February 21, 1916 dawned, the frigid air was shattered by the scream of heavy shells and the "whizz-bang" of anti-personnel weapons. More than two million shells fell on the forward French positions in the next 12 hours, after which the infantry began their attack.

For the first two days the German forces made relatively little headway, but on the 24th they broke through the main defensive line, taking 10,000 prisoners and capturing 65 artillery pieces. The infantry were preceded in their attacks by a rolling barrage from the immense number of guns at their disposal, which wrecked the defenses and drove the survivors under cover.

Between the awesome artillery barrage, the suddenness of the attack and the cold weather, the French were paralyzed. Some units broke and fled to the rear, leaving weak areas in the defenses through which the German assault troops advanced. The whole Verdun defense was collapsing. Something had to be done, and fast.

Verdun was supposed to be invincible—a French army commission in 1915 had confirmed this, and fired a general for saying otherwise. Yet on February 25, Fort Douaumont, a key component of the city's defenses, fell to German assault. This was a serious blow to French morale, though it could have been avoided had the garrison not been stripped to the bone. The defending infantry had broken under bombardment leaving a platoon of artillerymen as the only defenders. A nine-man German patrol found a way into the fort and discovered that it was virtually undefended. They led 300 of their fellows in and captured the keystone of the Verdun defenses almost without firing a shot.

PÉTAIN TAKES CHARGE

At the same time as Fort Douaumont was being captured by the enemy, General Pétain was arriving to take charge of the defences of Verdun. He found a desperate situation, with the only supply route into the city along a single road and a narrow-gauge railroad alongside it. This road, dubbed La Voie Sacrée, was Verdun's inadequate lifeline, and Pétain's first task was to improve it. Thousands of men worked to widen the road, allowing a less restricted flow of supplies into the city. By the time they had finished, something like 6,000 trucks could use the road every day, and over half a million troops, plus all their supplies, moved into and out of the city along it.

Pétain decided that units were only to serve 15-day tours in the trenches, to allow them time to rest and recuperate, so La Voie Sacrée saw an endless stream of units rotating to and from the front line. Although Pétain had improved the desperate logistics situation, things were still bad. The fighting ebbed somewhat at the very end of February, only to be resumed on March 5.

THE ATTACK IS RENEWED

A new German offensive was thrown in along the west bank of the Meuse, straight into the teeth of a well prepared defense. Pétain had deployed his best troops to meet this assault, and they were supported by a powerful concentration of artillery. This assault marked something of a turning point in the defense of Verdun. French gunners were not only inflicting horrific casualties on the attackers, but were conducting effective counterbattery fire against their

GENERAL PHILIPPE PÉTAIN earned a hero's reputation at Verdun and later in the war but came to be considered a traitor for collaborating with the Nazis in World War II.

BELOW: FRENCH PRISONERS taken early in the Verdun offensive are escorted to the rear. Early German successes stunned the French into passivity and it was some time before the garrison began to fight back effectively.

artillery. By the middle of April all the very heavy guns on the German side were out of action, and the German artillery had suffered another serious blow when a shell landed among almost half a million heavy artillery shells stockpiled in Spincourt forest. This caused the largest single explosion of the entire war.

The attacks continued through April and into May, and threatened to indeed "bleed the French army to death." However, gains were relatively slight and when Pétain was relieved by General Robert Nivelle, the French began to recover their offensive spirit.

NIVELLE TAKES OVER

Where Pétain had been the defender of Verdun and had prevented its fall, Nivelle took the offensive. The French slogan for Verdun was "Ils ne passeront pas!" ("They shall not pass!"), but Nivelle's aim was more than barring the door —he intended to kick the Germans back out.

At first Nivelle could do no more than Pétain; German attacks were still making gains and with Fort Douaumont in German hands the crux of the defense was now Fort Vaux. Vaux protected an area of high ground from which German guns would be able to fire directly into the city and, even more importantly, at the bridges over which all supplies into the city were fed. Fort Vaux became the target of

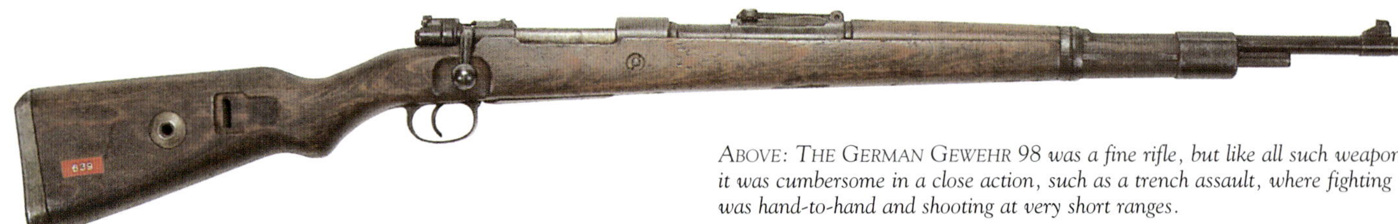

ABOVE: THE GERMAN GEWEHR 98 was a fine rifle, but like all such weapons it was cumbersome in a close action, such as a trench assault, where fighting was hand-to-hand and shooting at very short ranges.

German assaults, and on June 7 it fell to them. Nevertheless, the balance was shifting. Nivelle was an artillery officer, and under his command the French guns became more effective. Even as the Germans advanced toward the surviving forts, Souville and Tavannes, their casualties mounted.

Things hung in the balance throughout the end of June, and despite the opening of the Somme offensive on July 1, the Germans pushed onward, creeping ever closer to the city itself. On July 11 an attack actually reached Fort Souville, but its failure marked the end of German attempts to take Verdun. Thereafter they found themselves on the defensive as French counterattacks began to retake some of the ground lost earlier.

BELOW: A REMARKABLY CLEAN and spruce German soldier poses with rifle and grenade. He wears a gas mask typical of the type issued later in the war. Early versions were hurriedly improvised and only marginally effective.

Nivelle's position was improved by the Somme offensive, which was launched partly to reduce the pressure on Verdun. It did not succeed as an operation in its own right, but was successful in drawing in supplies and reinforcements that could otherwise be set against the defenders of Verdun. As the pressure eased, Nivelle launched counterattacks to drive the Germans out and retake the lost forts. The largest of these was on October 24, against Fort Douaumont and involved 170,000 infantry, 700 guns, and more than 150 aircraft. After this the French ground slowly forward, retaking Fort Vaux in early November. In the middle of December the German army retreated from Verdun, leaving what was left of it in French hands.

"THE MEATGRINDER"

By the end of the Verdun offensive, the Germans had indeed managed to cause vast French casualties—550,000 of them in fact. However, this was only achieved at a cost of 450,000

LEFT: FRENCH INFANTRY DIG IN somewhere in the Verdun sector, September 1916. The lot of the infantry was hard, living in wet and unsanitary conditions. This, combined with the horrendous casualties of the Verdun campaign, led to low morale and widespread rebellion among French troops in 1917.

casualties of their own. During the summer it was obvious that the cost was going to be very high, but the decision was taken to continue the offensive. One German casualty was the career of General Falkenhayn. On August 29 he was reassigned to command forces fighting against the Romanian army, which had joined the Allies the day before. This reassignment effectively represented a demotion. Falkenhayn was replaced by Hindenburg with Ludendorff as Quartermaster-General. Blaming Falkenhayn for the situation was perhaps unfair—he had realized as early as March that casualties were going to be too high, and pushed for an end to the operation. However, Crown Prince Wilhelm insisted on continuing.

The original German plan was reasonably sound—to attack something the enemy had to defend and drain his resources by artillery bombardment followed by infantry occupation of the devastated territory. However, the German army fell victim to "mission creep," and at some point the capture of Verdun became the objective of the operation. This was not the plan originally —the idea was to destroy the French army, not to seize a city —and Verdun was not worth half a million troops.

However, as the battle went on the objective shifted until the German army was being ground down in order to take a city it did not want or need. Winning the battle had become more important than the strategic objectives that inspired it. This led to losses that could not be sustained and were wholly unnecessary.

AFTERMATH

Virtually every French division on the Western Front passed through the Verdun meatgrinder. Rather fewer, but still large, numbers of German formations were rotated into the offensive. Massive casualties on both sides reduced the fighting power and the morale of both forces, and arguably it was the plight of Verdun that forced the Allies to make their costly Somme offensive, which in turn cost both sides vast numbers of lives. In the end, what was a workable plan did not succeed and the battle was inconclusive. The German failure to take Verdun was a boost to morale on the Allied side, and although the Somme offensive failed to achieve anything significant either, the German army did pull back to the Hindenburg Line in 1917.

The vast casualties at Verdun and the Somme were partly to blame for the collapse of French morale in 1917, the increasing cynicism and mistrust of commanders among the British troops, and the decline of the German army, which lost the best of its junior leaders in the bitter fighting of 1916. Verdun was perhaps a situation where failure to win in an operational context paved the way for defeat at the grand strategic level.

FRENCH INFANTRY SERGEANT

There were no great differences between the equipment used by troops on both sides in World War I; this French sergeant's equipment is similar to that used by his German foes. A metal helmet offers some protection against overhead shell bursts and he is armed with a rifle and a bayonet. He may have a grenade or two available.
Although heavy artillery hurled tons of shells across the trench lines and specialist weapons gradually emerged, including aircraft and armored vehicles, most of the great battles of the war were decided by infantrymen who doggedly clung to their positions or struggled to prize one another out of them.

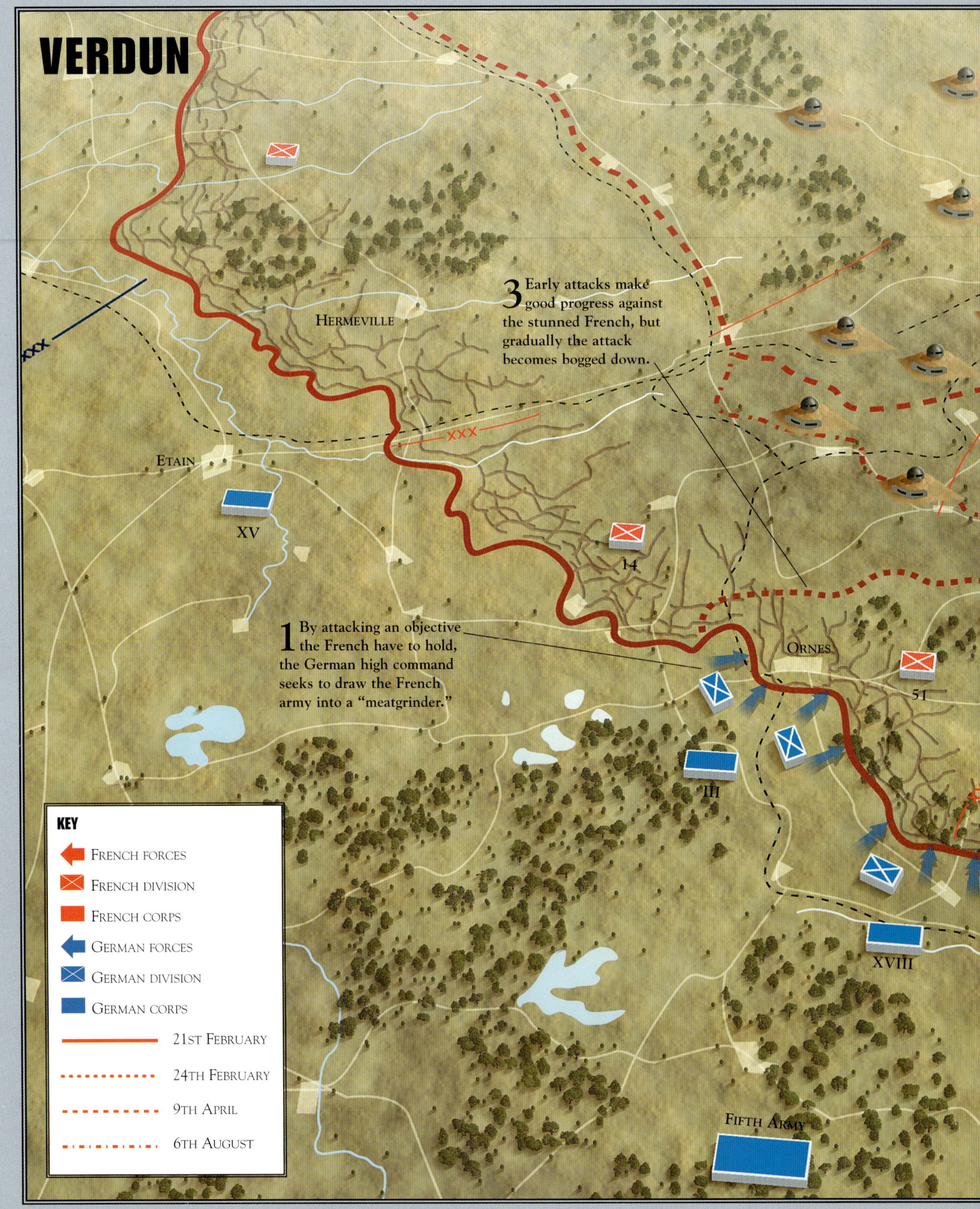
VERDUN
HERMEVILLE
ETAIN
XV
14
ORNES
51
III
XVIII
FIFTH ARMY
XXX
3 Early attacks make good progress against the stunned French, but gradually the attack becomes bogged down.
1 By attacking an objective the French have to hold, the German high command seeks to draw the French army into a "meatgrinder."
KEY
FRENCH FORCES
FRENCH DIVISION
FRENCH CORPS
GERMAN FORCES
GERMAN DIVISION
GERMAN CORPS
21ST FEBRUARY
24TH FEBRUARY
9TH APRIL
6TH AUGUST

4 The French cling to their positions, gaining strength as troops and supplies pour into the city down "La Voie Sacrée."
Verdun
5 Finally the French can go over to the offensive and begin to push the Germans out of their gained positions.
67
29
2 The battle opens with a massive artillery bombardment and infantry assault.
72
VI
VII
6 By the end of the battle, the lines are more or less back how they started. A million men lie dead for no gains by either side.

STALINGRAD 1942

The turning point of World War II, the battle of Stalingrad was a savage and bitter urban conflict in which tens of thousands of German and Soviet troops were killed. It was here that the Red Army proved it could not only hold off the Wehrmacht *in a defensive battle, but also take the offensive and defeat the seemingly invincible German war machine.*

Operation "Barbarossa," the German invasion of the Soviet Union, was the largest land invasion in history, pitting 3.6 million German troops and their allies against some three million Soviet troops in the western Soviet Union. Tactically and doctrinally superior, the Germans advanced further and faster than any other modern army, capturing some three million prisoners in the process. Yet the Soviet Union did not collapse as Hitler had so confidently predicted. Unclear strategic goals, logistical overstretch, unexpectedly tough Soviet resistance, and the terrible Russian winter meant the Germans failed to defeat their enemy decisively in 1941. Indeed the Red Army was able to launch a counteroffensive at Moscow on December 5–6, which

STALINGRAD FACTS

Who: The German Sixth Army under General Friedrich Paulus (1890–1957) against the Soviet Sixty-Second Army under General Vasily Chuikov (1900–82).

What: The Germans, bogged down in urban fighting where their superior mobile tactics were useless, were unable to take the city and were subsequently trapped by the Soviet counteroffensive and the Sixth Army surrendered.

Where: The city of Stalingrad on the Volga River, in the southern Soviet Union.

When: September 14, 1942 to February 2, 1943.

Why: The Germans sought to take Stalingrad to deal both a material and psychological blow to further Soviet resistance.

Outcome: Stalingrad was the turning point in the war on the Eastern Front, when the Soviets won their first major victory.

LEFT: A GERMAN MORTAR DETACHMENT prepares to move in the factory district of the city. Some of the fiercest fighting occurred around the factories, and the Red October factory was never captured in its entirety, despite numerous attacks.

ABOVE: GERMAN INFANTRY MANHANDLE a light infantry gun into position during the fighting in the north of Stalingrad. Light guns were often used against defended infantry positions.

caught the overextended, exhausted Germans unawares, pushing them back more than 100 miles (160km) in places before the line stabilized.

"Barbarossa" had cost the German army 1.1 million casualties. Only eight of the Eastern Army's 162 divisions were at full strength. Losses of vehicles were similarly high. By the spring of 1942 there was no question of resuming the offensive along the whole front, rather the Germans only had the resources for a single thrust. Stalin and the Soviet High Command anticipated that the Germans would resume their assault on Moscow and therefore massed their reserves in the area.

However, with the entry of the USA into the war in December 1941, Germany was now faced with the prospect of the opening of a Second Front and a long war of attrition. Thus Hitler decided to drive south toward the Transcaucasus and the oil fields, which supplied 90 percent of Soviet fuel. In the short term this would deny the Soviets fuel and in the long term provide resources for a drawn-out war against Britain and the USA. He set out this view in Führer Directive No. 41 on April 5, 1942, stating that: "All available forces will be concentrated on the main operations in the Southern sector, with the aim of destroying the enemy before the Don, in order to secure the Caucasian oil fields and the passes through the Caucasian Mountains themselves."

OPERATION "BLUE"

Operation "Blue," as the plan was code-named, was undertaken by Army Group South consisting of one million German and 300,000 allied troops, supported by *Luftflotte* 4 with 1,500 aircraft. There were two main axes of advance; Army Group A would drive for the Caucasus, while Army Group B would secure the northeastern flank of the advance along the Don and Volga rivers. "Blue" opened on June 28, 1942 and initially the Germans made rapid advances. Although they managed to inflict a number of telling defeats on the Soviets, Stalin had given permission to the Red Army to trade space for time and the retreat was made in reasonably good order.

Army Group A reached the oil fields at Maikop on August 9, but the advance slowed thereafter as resources were switched to Army Group B. Its main formation was Sixth Army led by Colonel-General Friedrich Paulus, which was pushing toward the city of Stalingrad, which sat on the major crossing point of the Volga River. On July 23, Hitler ordered that the city be taken. Militarily there were some sound reasons for capturing Stalingrad, because it would secure the flank of Army Group South and block an obvious launching point for a Soviet counterattack. However, the main motivations were political and psychological. The capture of the city that bore Stalin's name would be of huge value to the morale of both Germany and its allies.

STALINGRAD

Stalin also understood the importance of the city. On July 12 he established the Stalingrad Front made up of the Sixty-Second, Sixty-Third, and Sixty-Fourth Armies. A week later the city itself was put on an immediate war footing, but there was to be no mass evacuation of the population as Stalin believed that the troops would fight better for a "living city." On July 23 he issued Order No. 227 that the Red Army would take "Not a step back." German commanders noticed a definite stiffening of Soviet resistance, but they were able to batter their way through Sixty-Fourth Army and cross the Don on August 23.

The same day *Luftflotte* 4 launched a massive air raid on Stalingrad causing 30,000 casualties. The first German spearheads reached the Volga at Rynok and entered Stalingrad's northern suburbs. However, the advance on the city slowed in the face of poor terrain and desperate Soviet resistance. Thus the bulk of Paulus' army only reached the outskirts of central Stalingrad in early September. Herman Hoth's Fourth Panzer Army suffered similar difficulties in reaching the southern suburbs around about the same time.

THE OPPOSING FORCES

The Soviets estimated that about 170,000 men, 500 tanks, and 3,000 artillery pieces faced them on the 40-mile (64.3km) front around Stalingrad and its environs. They themselves could muster about 90,000 troops, 120 tanks, and 2,000 guns. A similar imbalance faced the defenders on the narrower front of the city itself, with the defending 54,000 strong Sixty-Second Army up against about 100,000 Germans. These numbers fluctuated throughout the battle due to losses and reinforcement, but the force ratios remained reasonably constant throughout. The main commanders were Paulus, an excellent staff officer and a capable solider, but probably unsuited to the bitter, attritional and messy urban battle that confronted him. Vasily Chuikov, commanding Sixty-Second Army, could not have contrasted more with the neat, fastidious Paulus. Tough, earthy, and bloody-minded, he was just the man for the grim task ahead of him and his troops.

Chuikov had also thought hard about how he was going to beat his adversary. The Soviets had chosen their ground well. In the campaigns that preceded Stalingrad, the Soviets had proved tactically and operationally inferior in the maneuver warfare that characterized the fighting on the wide, open spaces of the steppes. Key to German success had been the coordination of their infantry and armor and particularly close air support. They had, up to this point, eschewed urban combat in major conurbations. However, military, and particularly political, necessity meant the Germans would be fighting in an environment where their skills in maneuver were irrelevant. Even more importantly, their close air support would be considerably less effective. Conversely the Soviets' proven defensive tenacity, skill in close combat, and willingness to take losses would be a considerable advantage.

BELOW: TWO GERMAN SENIOR NCOs take shelter in a bomb crater in the initial fighting to capture the suburbs of Stalingrad. Both men are armed with MP38s, ideal weapons for close-quarter fighting in a built-up environment.

RED ARMY SOLDIER

This Red Army rifleman is wearing the new-pattern winter uniform introduced in 1941. By late 1942, his *telogreika*, a padded khaki jacket, was in common usage throughout the Red Army. He wears the matching padded pants, *valenki* felt boots and the so-called "fish-fur" cap or *shapka-ushank*, because the material it was manufactured from bore very little relation to real fur. He is armed with a PPSh-41 submachine gun. Ideal for urban warfare, the compact, robust PPSh-41 made up a large proportion of Soviet infantry weapons during the battle of Stalingrad.

THE MAMAYEV KURGAN

The Germans' first attempt to take the city opened on September 14 with a two-pronged assault by LI Corps on the center and south, supported by a push from the extreme southern suburbs by Fourth Panzer Army. The aim was to seize the dominating heights of the Mamayev Kurgan, where Chuikov had his headquarters, and capture the central landing stage, splitting the Sixty-Second Army in two and isolating it from resupply. An artillery strike knocked out Chuikov's HQ and the Germans pushed up over the

ABOVE: IN AN OBVIOUSLY STAGED PROPAGANDA photograph, a group of Soviet soldiers move cautiously through the ruins of Stalingrad amid the fighting during the fall of 1942. All are armed with Soviet PPSh-41 submachine guns.

Mamayev Kurgan toward Stalingrad No. 1 railroad station and the landing stages on the Volga River. Chuikov committed his last tactical reserves and pleaded with his Front commander, Colonel-General Yeremenko, to send him Major-General Rodmitstev's elite 13th Guards Division. The division had to fight its way from the landing stage to the station and onto the southeastern slopes of the Mamayev Kurgan. The station changed hands 15 times with the German 71st Division finally securing it on September 19. By then the 13th Guards, which had entered the battle 10,000 strong, could muster just 2,700 men.

In the south of the city, the Fourth Panzer Army met intense resistance, culminating in the battle around the grain silo, where 50 naval infantry and guardsmen held up three German divisions for several days. However, by September 26 Fourth Panzer Army had reached the Volga and split Sixty-Fourth Army from Chuikov's Sixty-Second Army. The Sixth Army held the crest of Mamayev Kurgan and made substantial gains in the center. Paulus could declare that "the battle flag of the Reich flies over the Stalingrad Party building," but the battle was far from over.

THE VOLGA CROSSINGS

Although the fighting continued around Mamayev Kurgan, the main German effort shifted into the factory district on September 27. The German attacks against the Soviet positions based around the industrial complexes of the Red October, Barrikady, and the Tractor factories, were intended to capture the landing stages behind them. Controlling the Volga was the key to the battle, because it was Sixty-Second Army's vital lifeline. Despite the tactical dominance of the Luftwaffe and the best efforts of the German artillery, they never managed to stop the flow of supplies and men across the river. After a week of bitter fighting the Sixth Army managed to cut off the Tractor Factory.

There was a lull in fighting and then the Germans redoubled their efforts in the factory district, finally capturing Barrikady and most of Red October. By the end of October they held 90 percent of the city and had all the Soviet-controlled areas under fire. But this had only been achieved at a massive cost. The Sixth Army was battered and exhausted and still it was not enough. The Red Army had taken the best the *Wehrmacht* could throw at it and still clung onto the banks of the Volga. On November 11, Paulus launched his last major assault, again in the factory district. It met with some success as German troops managed to reach the west bank of the river.

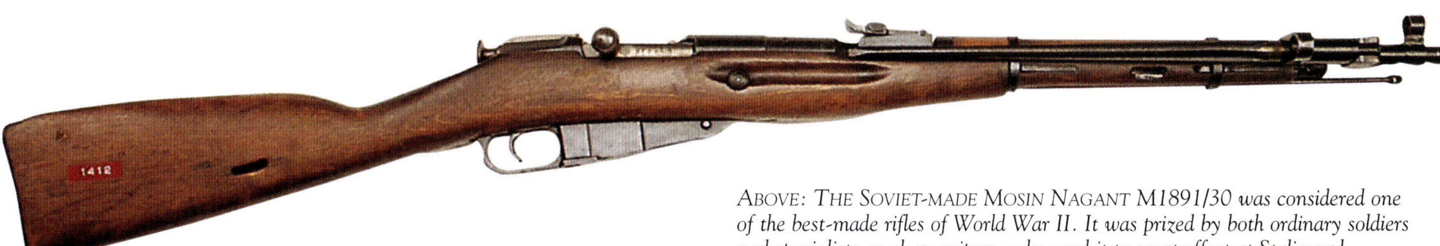

Above: The Soviet-made Mosin Nagant M1891/30 was considered one of the best-made rifles of World War II. It was prized by both ordinary soldiers and specialists, such as snipers, who used it to great effect at Stalingrad.

ZHUKHOV'S COUNTERATTACK

To maintain momentum over the seven weeks of bitter house-to-house fighting, the German command reduced the length of front held by Sixth Army and Fourth Panzer Army, leaving the flanks covered by Italian and Romanian forces. Stalin had given General Georgi Zhukhov (1896–1974) the task of organizing a counterattack to cut off the Sixth Army in Stalingrad. He built up one million men and 900 tanks in the hinterland behind the Volga, undetected by the Germans. Zhukov launched his assault, Operation "Uranus," on November 19. Three Armies of General Vatutin's South-West Front smashed through the Third Romanian Army and a day later Yeremenko's Stalingrad Front brushed aside the Fourth Romanian Army in the south. The two fronts met at Kalach on November 23, completing a perfect encirclement, that trapped roughly 250,000 German and Axis troops in the Stalingrad pocket.

Paulus requested permission to break out, but Hitler refused. The head of the Luftwaffe, Herman Göring, pledged to supply the Sixth Army by air and Hitler ordered Field Marshal von Manstein (1887–1973) to prepare a counter-attack to relieve Paulus' trapped troops. Operation "Winter Storm," which opened on December 12, needed to cover about 60 miles (97km). It was stopped 35 miles (59km) south of Stalingrad. Meanwhile Zhukov launched his offensive code-named "Little Saturn," threatening the entire German position in the south. "Winter Storm" was the Sixth Army's last hope. The Luftwaffe barely managed to land one-third of the supplies required and from January 10 the German position was increasingly constricted by Operation "Ring," General Rokossovsky's Don Front, and his attempt to close the pocket. Despite the futility of the struggle, the Soviets were impressed by the resilience of the German defenders. Nonetheless, they took about half the pocket in a week and after the last airfield fell, Paulus asked Hitler for permission to surrender. He was refused. By January 29 the Germans had been reduced to two pockets in the city, one around the Unimag Department Store in the center, the other in the factory district. On January 31 Hitler promoted Paulus to Field Marshal. The implications were obvious; no German commander of that rank had ever been captured alive. But Paulus surrendered that day; the northern pocket held out until February 2. German casualties at Stalingrad were about 200,000, with 110,000 of the Sixth Army going into Soviet captivity. Only 5,000 ever made it home.

AFTERMATH

Stalingrad marked a decisive turn in the war against Germany. The Soviet Army had outfought and out-thought the *Wehrmacht*. Although Germany would maintain a tactical edge, at Stalingrad, the Soviets demonstrated a superior grasp of the operational and strategic level of war. The Red Army had drawn the *Wehrmacht* into an attritional battle. Yet it had also been able to launch a large-scale, mobile "maneuverist" operation, which encircled and destroyed the Sixth Army. The victory at Stalingrad would be followed by many more.

Right: The Sturmgeschütz III assault gun was an important part of German offensive operations at Stalingrad. These turretless armored vehicles provided the assaulting German infantry with crucial support with direct fire on point targets, such as machine-gun emplacements and heavily defended buildings.

STALINGRAD
RYNOK
16 Pz
60 Mot
DZERSHINSKY
TRACTOR FACTORY
BARRIKADY FACTORY
388
100
75
71
295
5 Throughout October the Germans maintain their pressure in the factory district, bringing 90 percent of the city under their control.
3 On September 27 the Germans shift their main effort into the factory district in an attempt to capture the landing stages behind them.
1 The German LI Corps launches its first assault on the city on September 14 in an attempt to capture Mamayev Kurgan and the central landing stage by the river.
KEY
German movement
German infantry division
German armored division
German motorized division

6 The last major German attack begins on November 11. Eight days later the Soviets launch Operation "Uranus," cutting off the Sixth Army in the city.
4 The Soviets managed to maintain their supply lines across the Volga, providing the 62nd Army with just enough men and material to hang onto their foothold in the city.
2 The Fourth Panzer Army attacks in support in the south of the city, but are held up by fanatical resistance around the grain silo.
Red October factory
62nd Army HQ
Krasnaya Sloboda
Mamayev Kurgan
Pavlov's house
NKVD HQ
No. 1 Railroad Station
Grain Silo
Volga River
14 Pz
94
24 Pz
29 Mot

NORMANDY 1944

The battle for Normandy began with the spectacularly successful D-Day landings, thanks in no small part to an astounding campaign of deception that misled the German commanders completely. However, the breakout from Normandy was more problematic, and was only achieved after hard and costly fighting.

On the USA's entry into World War II in December 1941, the Americans and their British allies agreed on a policy of defeating Germany first, while containing the Japanese in the Pacific. It was clear that the defeat of Nazi Germany would eventually entail the landing of an Allied army on the European mainland. The British and Americans differed in how this should be achieved.

For the Americans the issue was simple. A large force should be landed in northwestern Europe to defeat the bulk of German forces and then march on Berlin. British military leaders, haunted by the slaughter of World War I and having experienced German military prowess, were less enthusiastic. They preferred a

NORMANDY FACTS

Who: American, British, Canadian, and French forces under the supreme command of General Dwight D. Eisenhower (1890–1969) against the German armies in the West commanded by Field Marshal Gerd von Rundstedt (1875–1953).

What: After the largest amphibious landings in military history, the Allies were able to establish themselves on the Continent and break out of Normandy after harder-than-expected fighting.

Where: The Normandy peninsula in western France.

When: June 6–August 19, 1944.

Why: The Allies sought to establish a Second Front, liberate Western Europe, and drive on into Nazi Germany.

Outcome: The German Army in Normandy was effectively destroyed and the Allies advanced east toward the German border.

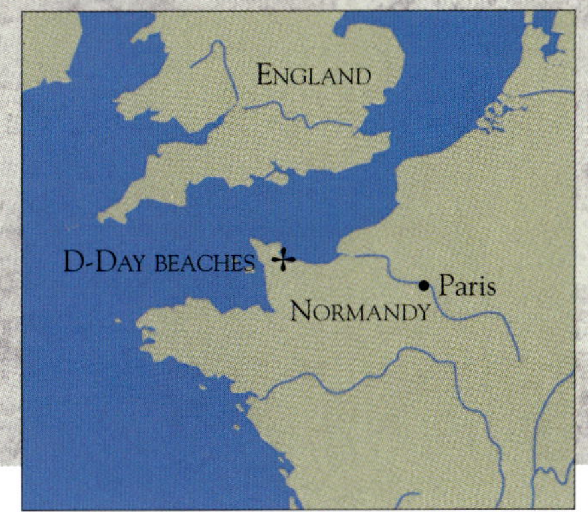

LEFT: AMERICAN INFANTRY WADE ASHORE on Omaha Beach. These are almost certainly part of a later wave of troops to land, because they are not encountering the deathly fire experienced by the earlier waves. Despite the low-lying cloud apparent in this photograph, the weather cleared in the afternoon, allowing Allied airpower to dominate the battlefield.

strategy of dispersing German strength by continuing the campaign in the Mediterranean. For a while the British policy prevailed, but at the Casablanca Conference of January 1943, the British were forced to accept American military logic and agree to a major military landing in France. In May a provisional date for the operation, now code-named "Overlord," was set for May 1, 1944.

OPERATION "OVERLORD"

The prospect of transporting enough troops across the English Channel to establish and hold a beachhead and then reinforcing them faster than the Germans could bolster their own forces was a daunting task. Eschewing the most direct route across the Straits of Dover, the planners decided to land in Normandy. This was largely because it was within the range of Allied air cover, had firm and sheltered beaches, and was close to Cherbourg, a major port. General Dwight D. Eisenhower was appointed Supreme Commander with General Bernard Montgomery (1887–1976) as the commander of the invasion's land forces. They immediately altered the original plan, by widening the beachhead and expanding the initial amphibious assault from three divisions to five, supported by various commando and Ranger units, with three airborne divisions dropped inland to secure the flanks. They would be rapidly followed by the rest of the U.S. First Army under General Omar Bradley (1893–1981) and the British Second Army commanded by General Sir Miles Dempsey (1896–1969). By late 1943, it was clear to the Germans that an Anglo-American invasion

RIGHT: GENERAL EISENHOWER gives a pep talk to members of the 101st Airborne prior to their drop on the Normandy countryside.

BELOW: A BRITISH SERGEANT SMILES for the camera as infantry form up on Sword Beach, ready to support the armor that is preparing to move off. The men have canvas covers for the bolts of their rifles, to protect them from the seawater and sand as they landed.

would come; it was just a question of when and where. Most of the German commanders, Hitler included, believed that the Allies would attempt to land on the Pas de Calais. Field Marshal von Rundstedt, the German Commander-in-Chief in the West, had 58 divisions under his command, but half of these were static, tied to stretches of coastal defenses. Key to the defeat of any Allied invasion, was his nine panzer and one panzergrenadier divisions. However, he disagreed with his subordinate Field Marshal Erwin Rommel (1891–1944), commander of Army Group B, made up of Fifteenth Army in the Pas de Calais and Seventh Army protecting Normandy, as to how that armor should be used. Von Rundstedt and General von Schweppenburg, commander of Panzer Group West, wanted the armor held back to deliver a crushing counterattack. Rommel felt this would be impossible given Allied control of the air. He believed that the Germans had to defeat the invasion on the beaches and thus he wanted the armor deployed as close to the beaches as possible. Hitler's solution was a compromise. In Normandy this meant only one panzer division, the 21st, was located close to the coast with the rest, Panzer Lehr and 12th SS Panzer, held further back. This left both commanders dissatisfied; Rommel felt his forward defences were inadequate and Von Rundstedt believed his panzer reserve was too small.

SHERMAN DD TANK

The DD (Duplex Drive) Sherman was the amphibious version of the main Anglo-American tank. A collapsible fabric screen and inflatable pillars and two small propellers allowed the tank to "swim." Once it was ashore, the screen could be collapsed and the DD Sherman could function as a normal tank.

DECEPTION PLANS

For "Overlord" to succeed, the Allies had to train and then assemble their forces in southern England. The Air Commander-in-Chief, Air Chief Marshal Leigh-Mallory (1892–1944) had to ensure air superiority over the beaches and hamper German supply and reinforcement capabilities. The Allied air forces targeted the French transportation system, but in such a way so as not to draw attention to Normandy. An intricate deception plan, Operation "Fortitude" sought to convince the Germans that, firstly, the Pas de Calais was the intended target and, secondly, the actual invasion of Normandy was simply a diversion. This succeeded perfectly.

The Allies assembled a vast invasion fleet of nearly 7,000 warships, transports, and support vessels to escort and provide fire support or carry the 130,000 troops across the Channel. During June 5, after a 24-hour delay due to bad weather, the fleet assembled off the south coast of England and began to sail south toward the six landing beaches in Normandy, designated from west to east, "Utah," "Omaha," "Gold," "Juno," and "Sword." They were passed overhead by the first Allied bombers en route to attack the German defenses. These were followed from 11:30 P.M. by the transport planes taking the 17,000 airborne troops to drop zones to the east and west of the beaches.

D-DAY

The Battle of Normandy opened just after midnight on June 6 as the British 6th Airborne Division landed northeast of Caen. The first troops into action were glider-borne troops of 2nd Oxford and Buckinghamshire Light Infantry, who quickly secured the bridges over the Caen canal and the Orne River. Other units of the 6th Airborne captured several bridges over the Orne, overran the Melville Battery, and secured the invasion's left flank by holding the Ranville-Hérouvillette area. Meanwhile at about 1 A.M. the

RIGHT: JUST 41FT (12.5M) in length, the LCA (landing craft assault) were some of the smaller craft used to transport troops on D-Day, carrying about 30 personnel.

American paratroops of the 82nd and 101st Airborne Divisions jumped into the marshy terrain around the westernmost landing beach "Utah." The paratroopers did much to confuse the German response, which was not helped by the fact that Rommel was on leave. "Fortitude" had also ensured that the Germans continued to expect the main invasion in the Pas de Calais even several days after D-Day and thus held back their reserves.

Two hours later 1,900 bombers began attacking the German defenses in the landing area and as dawn approached the naval bombardment opened. At 6:30 A.M. the Americans of 4th Division began their run-in at "Utah" beach; the Canadians attacking "Juno" beach would land as late as 7:45 A.M. as a result of tidal conditions. On "Utah" the Americans quickly established themselves ashore, advanced across the waterlogged terrain behind the beach and linked up with airborne forces in the area. This was achieved for the cost of just under 200 casualties.

Things went rather less well on "Omaha" beach. Allied intelligence had failed to notice that the defending regiment of the 716th Division, a static formation, had been reinforced by two regiments of the veteran 352nd Division. These men largely survived the preparatory bombardment unscathed. On top of this the poor weather conditions meant that only five of the 32 DD swimming Sherman tanks and very few of the Americans' supporting combat engineers made it ashore. The assaulting troops of 1st Infantry and 29th National Guard Divisions took terrible losses to the well dug-in German troops. By the end of the day they had secured a tenuous foothold that was no deeper than 2,000 yards (1.8km) at the cost of more than 2,000 casualties. "Gold" was the westernmost Anglo-Canadian beach. It was assaulted by the British 50th (Northumbrian) Division. Unlike the Americans, the British were supported by a variety of specialized armored fighting vehicles, such as AVRE assault tanks, to breach defenses, and Sherman Crab flail tanks, designed to clear minefields, in addition to their DD tanks. By the end of the day, 50th Division had managed to push 4 miles (6.4km) inland while 47 Commando struck westward toward the Americans on Omaha.

LEFT: THIS U.S. INFANTRY CAPTAIN carries an M1 Carbine. The carbine was designed for specialist troops, such as drivers and machine gunners, but such was its lightness and ease of handling it became popular with front-line troops.

Meanwhile the 3rd Canadian Infantry Division landed on "Juno," the central British-Canadian beach. They met particularly strong resistance and were hampered by the loss of many landing craft to submerged obstacles. It took the Canadians an hour and a quarter of hard fighting to secure the first exits from the beach. They also managed to push about 4 miles (6.4km) inland by the end of the day.

On "Sword" the most easterly beach, effective fire support suppressed the enemy defenses and most of the landing craft taking ashore the 3rd Infantry Division made the run-in undamaged. However, due to the bad weather the incoming tide was higher than expected, which meant the craft were deposited among the German submerged beach obstacles that the Allies had expected to be visible. Landing higher up the beach than expected did have the advantage of reducing the amount of ground the infantry had to cross, but in the confined space of the beach armored vehicles soon became congested, hampering the British attempt to push inland. The 3rd Division was tasked with linking up with 6th Airborne on the Orne River, which 1st Special Service Brigade and 8th Brigade achieved reasonably quickly. However, the capture of Caen, which was also scheduled for the first day, proved a little more difficult. The drive on the city was disrupted by a counter-attack by 21st Panzer. The German division drove straight into the gap between "Juno" and "Sword" beaches, but faltered in the face of British anti-tank and tank gunnery.

THE BATTLE FOR CAEN

Caen had not fallen, but otherwise it had been a remarkably successful day. The Allies had achieved massive strategic surprise and landed over 130,000 men at the cost of about 6,000 U.S. and 4,300 British and Canadian casualties. The Germans had failed to drive them back into the sea and over the next few days the beachheads were linked up and resources poured into the Normandy pocket. By D-Day +6 about 330,000 men, 55,000 vehicles, and 104,000 tons of supplies had been landed. However, a rapid break-out did not follow. The Americans pushed up into the Cotentin Peninsula towards Cherbourg, while British and Canadians concentrated on the capture of Caen. Montgomery's plan for Normandy was for the British to tie down the weight of German resources, particularly their armor, to give the Americans the opportunity to break-out in the face of

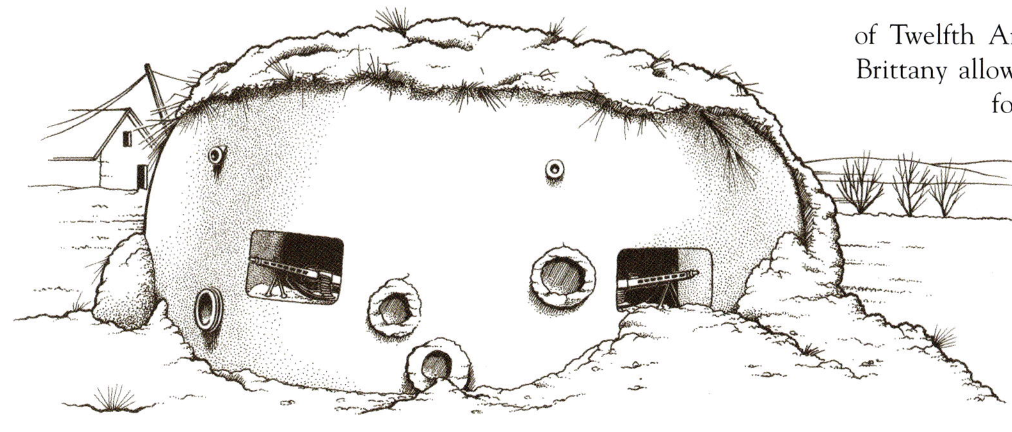

ABOVE: LIKE THIS MACHINE-GUN EMPLACEMENT, some of the defenses on the Atlantic Wall had been taken from the French Maginot Line and other obstacles built by the Belgians and Dutch in the late 1930s. Many of these old defenses proved very effective against the advancing Allies.

weaker resistance. This was a reasonable enough strategy but his reputation with his allies and posterity was not well served by his overconfident predictions of success for the operations to capture Caen. A Canadian push on the city on June 7 floundered in the face of the arrival of 12th SS Panzer Division, a broad outflanking maneuver was stopped at Villers-Bocage on June 12, and the carefully prepared Operation "Epsom" from June 25–30 failed in the face of desperate German counterattacks. The city finally fell on July 8. Even then the British failed to break-out toward Falaise and took massive losses, particularly in tanks, during Operation "Goodwood" from July 18–20.

THE BREAKOUT

Nonetheless these operations had had the desired effect of sucking the German armored forces into a battle of attrition on the western side of the lodgment. The German commanders had hoped to husband their panzer divisions for a counterattack that would drive the Allies into the sea, but had been forced to fritter these resources away in a desperate attempt to shore up the line in the face of constant British pressure. Meanwhile the Americans had managed to capture Cherbourg and as "Goodwood" drew in the bulk of German armor in Normandy, they prepared an offensive to capitalize on the weakened German line in front of them. This would be the crowning achievement of the campaign.

On the morning of July 25 a massive air bombardment heralded the opening of Operation "Cobra." American infantry and armor broke through the German lines and headed south for Coutances. After two days' fighting it was clear that the Americans had destroyed the Germans' left flank and opened up the way into Brittany. On August 1, the U.S. Third Army under General George Patton (1885–1945) became operational and Bradley handed 1st Army over to General Hodges, stepping up to take command of Twelfth Army Group. Lack of resistance in Brittany allowed Patton to shift the bulk of his forces westward. Despite the imminent collapse of the German position, Hitler insisted on a counter-offensive, which was launched against the U.S. First Army in the Mortain area on August 7, but they only succeeded in pushing their remaining armor further westward into a pocket that was rapidly closing around them. This gave Bradley the idea of pushing Patton's troops at Le Mans northward, while the Canadians drove south toward Falaise, a move that might trap an estimated 21 German divisions in the pocket. Montgomery immediately approved and although the two armies did not meet until August 19, some 10,000 Germans were killed and 50,000 captured. About 20,000 escaped. The battle for Normandy was over.

AFTERMATH

The Normandy Landings were an extraordinary achievement, easily the largest amphibious operation in history. The Allies had managed to establish themselves on a hostile coastline and reinforce their position faster than their enemy, who relied on the comprehensive road and rail network of northwestern Europe. Much of the success was down to an impressive logistical effort by the Allies and the importance of air power in hampering the German response. The landings did not lead to a rapid break-out and collapse of the German position in the west, but the Normandy Campaign caused losses to the Germans in terms of men and material and the establishment, at last, of the Second Front meant that Germany's strategic position was now untenable.

RIGHT: AN MG42 MACHINE GUNNER, of the Waffen-SS "Hitler Jugend" Division. This division was brought in as reinforcements to stem the Allied advance.

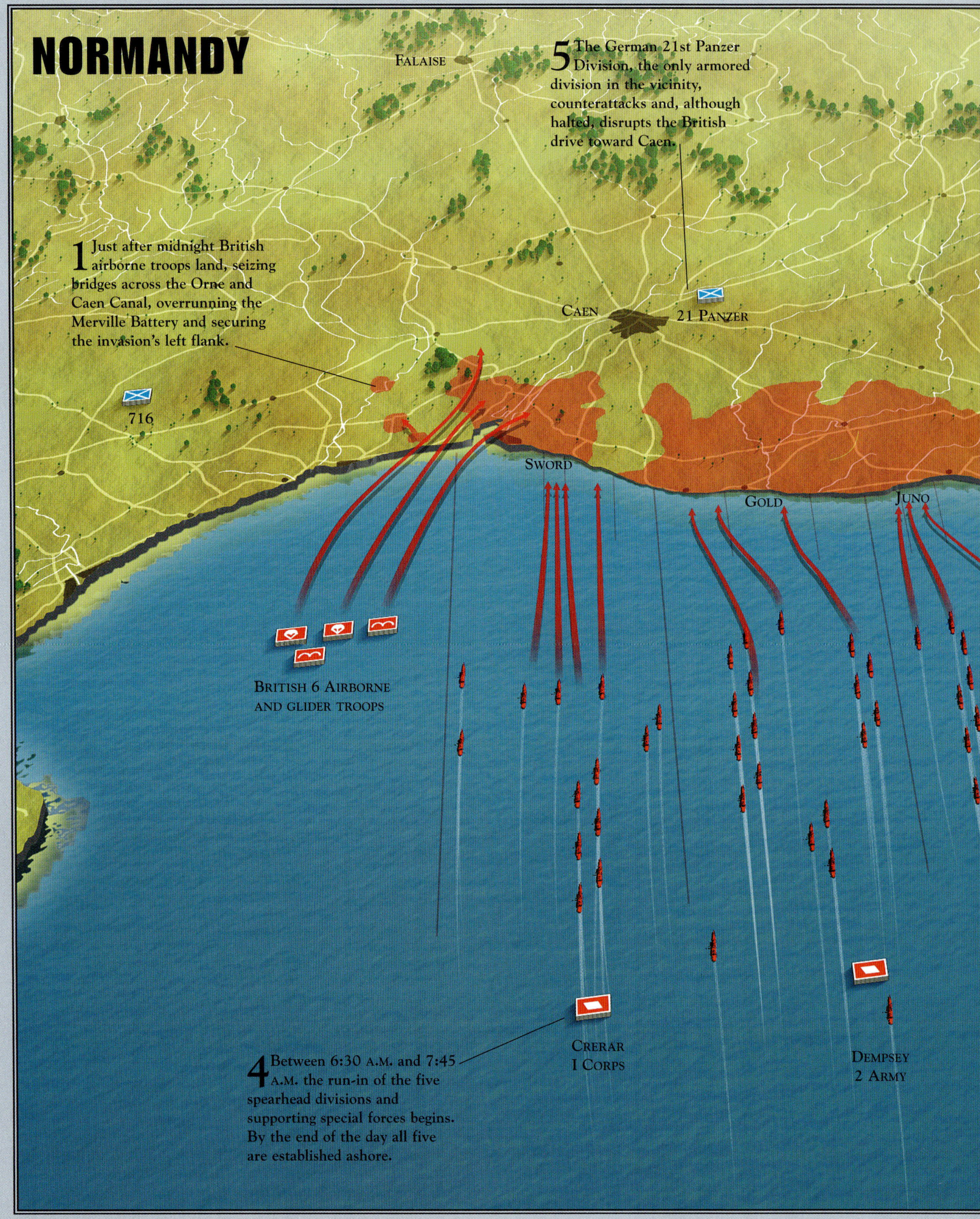
NORMANDY
FALAISE
5 The German 21st Panzer Division, the only armored division in the vicinity, counterattacks and, although halted, disrupts the British drive toward Caen.
1 Just after midnight British airborne troops land, seizing bridges across the Orne and Caen Canal, overrunning the Merville Battery and securing the invasion's left flank.
CAEN
21 PANZER
716
SWORD
GOLD
JUNO
BRITISH 6 AIRBORNE AND GLIDER TROOPS
4 Between 6:30 A.M. and 7:45 A.M. the run-in of the five spearhead divisions and supporting special forces begins. By the end of the day all five are established ashore.
CRERAR
I CORPS
DEMPSEY
2 ARMY

3 At 3 A.M., 1,900 Allied bombers attack the German defenses in the landing area followed by a naval bombardment from seven battleships, 18 cruisers, 43 destroyers, and a monitor.
2 At 1 A.M. U.S. airborne troops land to the west of Utah beach to secure the western flank of the invasion beaches.
91
COUTANCE
ST. LÔ
709
CARENTAN
XXX
AYEUX
OMAHA
UTAH
243
U.S. 82 AND 101 AIRBORNE
GEROW V CORPS
COLLINS VII CORPS
BUCKNALL XXX CORPS
BRADLEY 1 ARMY
KEY
ALLIED FORCES
ALLIED DIVISION
ALLIED ARMOR
GERMAN FORCES
GERMAN DIVISION

INDEX